The Chappy Ferry Book

Back and Forth Between Two Worlds ~ 527 Feet Apart

story by TOM DUNLOP | photos by ALISON SHAW

VINEYARD STORIES
Edgartown, Massachusetts

Historical photos: Courtesy of the Martha's Vineyard Museum
Pages: 8, 9, 11, 12, 13, 15, 19, 20, 22, 23, 24, 25, 27, 31,
32, 33, 35, 36, 37, 38, 39, 40, 42, 43, 44, 46, 78, 90, and 101.

Historical photo Courtesy of the Martha's Vineyard
Camp-Meeting Association: Page 17

Back Cover: The *City of Chappaquiddick* heads
to Chappy Point after World War II.

Published by Vineyard Stories
52 Bold Meadow Road
Edgartown, Massachusetts 02539

508-221-2338

www.vineyardstories.com

Library of Congress Number: 2011945420

ISBN: 9780-9849136-0-2

Book Design: Jill Dible, Atlanta, Georgia

Editor: Jan Pogue, Vineyard Stories

Printed in China

Dedicated to the Chappy ferry owners, captains, and crew—past, present, and future.

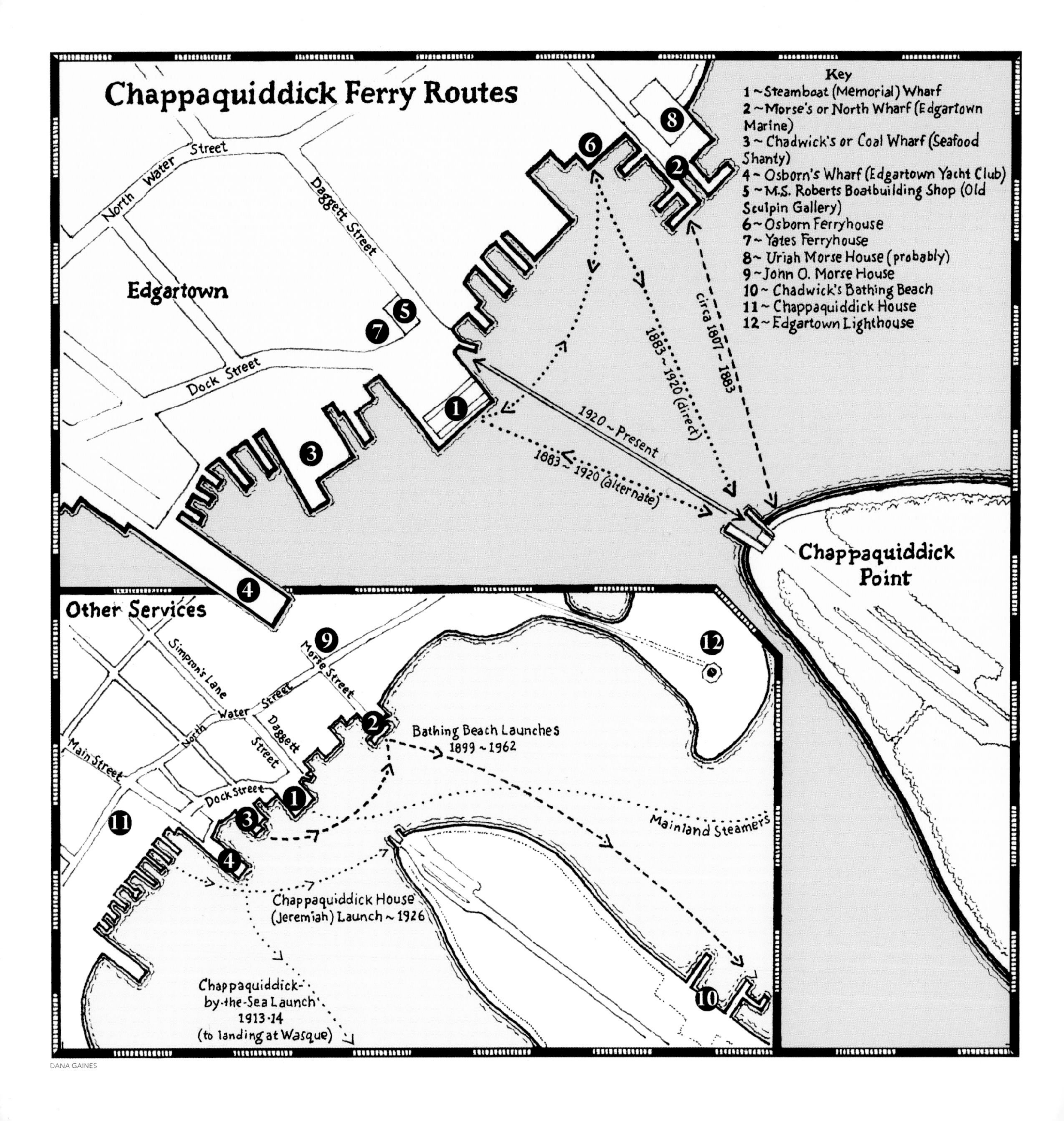
Chappaquiddick Ferry Routes
Key
1 ~ Steamboat (Memorial) Wharf
2 ~ Morse's or North Wharf (Edgartown Marine)
3 ~ Chadwick's or Coal Wharf (Seafood Shanty)
4 ~ Osborn's Wharf (Edgartown Yacht Club)
5 ~ M.S. Roberts Boatbuilding Shop (Old Sculpin Gallery)
6 ~ Osborn Ferryhouse
7 ~ Yates Ferryhouse
8 ~ Uriah Morse House (probably)
9 ~ John O. Morse House
10 ~ Chadwick's Bathing Beach
11 ~ Chappaquiddick House
12 ~ Edgartown Lighthouse
North Water Street
Daggett Street
Edgartown
Dock Street
1883 ~ 1920 (direct)
Circa 1807 ~ 1883
1920 ~ Present
1883 ~ 1920 (alternate)
Chappaquiddick Point
Other Services
Simpson's Lane
Morse Street
North Water Street
Daggett Street
Main Street
Dock Street
Bathing Beach Launches 1899 ~ 1962
Mainland Steamers
Chappaquiddick House (Jeremiah) Launch ~ 1926
Chappaquiddick-by-the-Sea Launch 1913-14 (to landing at Wasque)

DANA GAINES

TABLE OF CONTENTS

FERRY
CROSSING
EDGARTOWN

Before the Beginning

Circa Twenty-one Thousand Years Ago to 1807

Before there can be a ferry between Edgartown and Chappaquiddick there must be islands, and before there can be islands there must be ice.

In this part of the world, the ice comes from what is now southeastern Canada, a mountain of it more than a mile high at its highest. It grinds south over tens of thousands of years, advancing by feet and inches in the whistling, merciless cold of the long winter months, retreating when it briefly warms above freezing in what passes for summer.

The Atlantic Ocean, in this epoch, lies hundreds of miles to the south and east. The seafloor is an arid coastal plain. The glacier bulldozes its way onto the landscape in three lobes, each one steep, gray, and many miles wide.

To the west, one lobe piles up the rocky backbone of what will one day become western Martha's Vineyard. Far to the east, another lobe excavates the Great South Channel, beneath what is now the ocean. The middle lobe leaves behind the rock and muck that begin to form the eastern Vineyard and all of Nantucket—and between them the future island of Chappaquiddick.

About twenty-one thousand years ago, meltwater from the departing ice begins to sweep away just enough of the slag to separate the Chappy rock heap from the Vineyard and Nantucket rock heaps to either side of it. When ancestors to the modern Wampanoags reach these dump sites from what is now the mainland, after most of the glacial torrent drains away into the rising sea, Chappaquiddick may already look islandlike to them, a jumble of rubble notably separated from the rubble all around it.

These pioneers from Asia and the continent arrive twelve or thirteen thousand years ago. They move seasonally across the hills and plains, well before the ocean swamps the basins that become Vineyard and Nantucket sounds.

But the rise of the sea follows rapidly in geologic time. By six thousand years ago it surrounds the Islands, including Chappaquiddick. Chappy eventually comes

Chappaquiddick landscape viewed from Wasque, circa 1890.

to look like a distorted triangle of about thirty-eight hundred acres, with a barrier beach sweeping protectively around the top.

Though Martha's Vineyard is seventeen times larger than Chappaquiddick, neighboring Chappy defends much of the eastern half of the Vineyard from the Atlantic to the south and gales from the north and east. On a map, however, Chappaquiddick itself looks rather delicate, as much an island of bays, ponds, and inlets as of land.

Accounting for the modern spelling, this is what chappaquiddick *means in the Algonquin language: "at the separated island."*

Yet it's truly an island only about half the time. From the south shore of the Vineyard, a coastal beach runs narrowly eastward until it tethers itself to the south shore of Chappaquiddick, making Chappy a peninsula of the larger Island for decades at a stretch.

But when great storms strike, this barrier beach sometimes blows open to the sea, severing Chappy from the rest of the Vineyard and making it an island of its own. Accounting for the modern spelling, this is what *chappaquiddick* means in the Algonquin language: "at the separated island."

From the windy shores and choppy waters, the first Chappaquiddick natives fish and whale. From Chappy bays and ponds they harvest abundant beds of shellfish. In the forests they hunt, and on the hilly, shrubby ground they set fires to open the land for farming and berry picking.

In 1642 a company of perhaps thirty Englishmen settles on the wooded shoreline of what they call Martha's Vineyard, just across the harbor entrance from Chappaquiddick Point.

Led by Thomas Mayhew Sr., an entrepreneur from the Massachusetts Bay Colony, these newcomers covet the independence that life on the offshore Vineyard offers them.

They also come to covet Chappaquiddick.

The colonists declare Chappy to be part of the little Vineyard settlement they first call Great Harbour and later Edgartown. They swim cattle across the harbor to graze free-range on Chappaquiddick from late fall to early spring, the sheep and cows ravaging native cornfields and disturbing the Wampanoag hunting grounds.

They also introduce smallpox and other diseases for which the natives have no immunity; the tribal population on Chappaquiddick, which probably numbers about 150 when the settlers arrive, is likely cut in half within two decades.

The first white family moves onto Chappy before 1750. By 1807, when a theologian from Boston named James Freeman tours the Vineyard and Chappaquiddick, there are thirty-eight English families living on the island and sixty-five Chappaquiddick Wampanoags, most making do on a small parcel of land set off for them at North Neck.

James describes Chappaquiddick as an island of scrubby oaks and sandy but in places productive soil, with natives harvesting inexhaustible beds of quahaugs in Cape Pogue Pond. He follows the shoreline west until he comes to a "low, flat beach, called Chappaquiddick Point," which "approaches the wharves of Old Town"—Edgartown—"at a distance of forty rods," or 660 feet.

Then in a single sentence—more an afterthought than anything else—James introduces the one manmade enterprise from his time on Chappaquiddick that he would recognize, without much more explanation, in ours: "Over this narrow strait," he writes, "a ferry boat passes from one Island to the other."

It is the first reference that we know of to the Chappaquiddick ferry. From this footnote begins the lively story of the oldest business on the waters of Martha's Vineyard. From it, too, begins a drama that—incredibly enough—does its part to alter the political affairs of a nation and the popular culture of a planet.

And the first man to run it is a southerner who soon finds his little rowboat ferry mixed up fearfully in something like a religious war.

Population on Chappaquiddick

- Early 1660s: Seventy-five Wampanoags, estimated

MARTHA'S VINEYARD MUSEUM

Chappy schoolhouse, circa 1890.

CHAPTER 1

Uriah Morse

Circa 1807–1835

The first trip of the Chappaquiddick ferry on record is one that Uriah Morse does not dare make.

Though he comes rather hazily into the whole picture of Vineyard history, Uriah is the first Chappy ferryman identified by name, and evidence suggests he is the man who starts the service.

Born in Beaufort, North Carolina, in 1772, Uriah is likely the grandson of Joseph Morse Sr., who holds lucrative whaling rights on the nearby barrier islands known as the Shackleford Banks.

The trade of his father, Theodore, is unknown, as is the reason Uriah sets off for faraway Nantucket about the time he turns twenty. From there in 1793 he ships as a cooper, or barrel maker, aboard the whaler *Mary Ann*, under the command of Captain Tristram Folger, which hunts off the coast of Brazil. It is the only whaling voyage Uriah ever makes.

In 1796 he is married to Prudence Fish and living in Edgartown—a natural move for a cooper, since Edgartown, a village of whaling masters, is also growing rich off of a problem Nantucket never quite manages to solve.

A sandbar at the entrance to Nantucket Harbor resists dredging and, in the time of Uriah Morse, prevents the largest Nantucket whaling ships, heavily laden with oil after profitable voyages around the world, from sailing the last mile home. Instead these ships often sail into nearby Edgartown, where they unload their catches, make repairs, and provision for their next trips.

Edgartown waterfront from Chappy Point, circa 1835.

MARTHA'S VINEYARD MUSEUM

The breeze off the harbor smells of shellfish, smoked herring, and whale oil.

Casks of whale oil line the wharves in Edgartown, and Uriah works on a waterfront busy with bakers and grocers, makers of shoes and beaver hats, blacksmiths and shipwrights, riggers and sailmakers. The breeze off the harbor smells of shellfish, smoked herring, and whale oil.

"More than one old boy will remember the scoldings he received because he spoiled his trousers with gurry when searching for coacoanuts and other things in the hold of some newly arrived ship," Henry Baylies, an Edgartown native, writes years afterward.

Sailors sing as they hoist barrels onto the wharves and wander the streets restlessly between sailings. There are inns, billiard rooms, and three taverns in the village, and to earn a little extra income as they start a family, Uriah and Prudence open a dance hall on the main floor of the home they either buy or build near the entrance to the harbor at the north end of town.

Uriah takes up boatbuilding as well as coopering one floor below the home and dance hall, and when he looks east, a few hundred feet across the harbor entrance, he realizes that Chappaquiddick has also become a place of business and industry.

Poucha Pond and Nantucket Sound as seen from Chappaquiddick, circa 1890.

MARTHA'S VINEYARD MUSEUM

Meetinghouse at Sampson's Hill, Chappaquiddick, circa 1886.

MARTHA'S VINEYARD MUSEUM

In these busy times, Uriah realizes, not everyone who wants to do business on Chappy owns a boat.

Dealers and fishermen sail from as far away as Connecticut to buy quahaugs from Chappaquiddick Indians who harvest them in Cape Pogue Pond. Pilots at Wasque, the distant southeastern elbow of Chappaquiddick, launch sharp-ended surfboats into breaking Atlantic seas and row miles out to whalers and merchant ships to guide them safely into Edgartown.

There is a mariner's church—soon to become an all-purpose meetinghouse—on Sampson's Hill, at ninety-four feet the highest peak on the island. And if there is not yet a saltworks on Chappaquiddick Point as Uriah gazes across the channel in these early years of the nineteenth century, a town entrepreneur named James Bunting will soon build a profitable one.

Back home in North Carolina, Uriah recalls, two relatives run ferries across the coastal waterways of Beaufort, and in these increasingly busy times not everyone who wants to do business on Chappy owns a boat. Among them in the first years of the 1800s, Uriah counts the charismatic pastors—Methodist and Baptist—who are suddenly coming over from the mainland to hold nighttime revival meetings in the town.

These evangelists challenge the official religion of Edgartown, which arrived from England with the Mayhew settlers in 1642 and is distinctly puritanical in its beliefs: Man has no free will, this Congregational faith declares. Only the elect will be saved. Behave as if you are among them, but know that you can do nothing to change God's mind if he has determined from the start that you aren't among the chosen.

The charismatic new ministers from the mainland proclaim the opposite: Man can choose between doing right and wrong; salvation is up to each person and

No Signs of Good on Chappaquiddick

"Monday, visited Chappaquiddick, a small island, which is a part of Edgartown. I preached. There appeared no signs of good. . . ."

—From the autobiography of "Reformation" John Adams, an itinerant Methodist evangelist, June 1821

comes only through good works and conversion to Christ. At late-night meetings in private Edgartown homes that would be secret if they were not also so thunderously noisy, converts to the new religion cry out for salvation, envision balls of fire rolling through the house, hear voices, speak in tongues, scream, shudder, clap, and bawl. Some—freshly born again—fall to the floor in a faint.

Defenders of the old faith react violently to the cultlike incursions of the vigorous new one. They throw stones, mud, and even the carcasses of dead cats into the rooms where the Methodists and Baptists meet. They bust through doors, disrupt sermons, and rough up the visiting preachers, who report to their followers that, even in daylight, they walk the streets of Edgartown in fear of their lives.

What they need, agree the converts, is a place where they can worship safely removed from the threatening hand of the oppressor. They look across the harbor and see the perfect refuge in Chappaquiddick—an "outpost," writes the Reverend Hebron Vincent of Edgartown, where practitioners of the new "experimental religion" can "worship in greater quietness."

MARTHA'S VINEYARD MUSEUM

Hebron Vincent

Uriah himself wants nothing to do with evangelical Methodism—it takes a stern line against dance halls, among other things—but he sees how many people want to go to Chappy for reasons of business or religion, and he seizes the opportunity before him. By 1807 Uriah and Prudence Morse have a daughter, four sons, and—in all likelihood—the first ferry service to Chappaquiddick.

The Morse home and boatbuilding and coopering shop lie just across the harbor from Chappaquiddick Point. Uriah owns at least one skiff, and it is a simple thing to step away from his labors to row an entrepreneur—or proselyte—to Chappy whenever one appears at his door . . . and to catch sight of one over on Chappaquiddick Point whenever one shows up, looking for a ride back to Edgartown.

Easy extra money at two cents per passenger and no worries to speak of—until that day four years later when Uriah looks across the harbor entrance and sees the Reverend Erastus Otis, the first Methodist preacher to come to Edgartown, standing on the Point in a rainstorm.

SIDNEY N. RIGGS

Full-rigged ship, mid-1800s.

Uriah pulls on a coat, shoulders his oars, and walks down to the beach. On reaching his rowboat he hears hooting, yelling, and laughter. He looks up and down the waterfront, and what he sees on the wharves and piers astonishes him. Scores of Edgartown men, perhaps even hundreds if you add in the roughneck crewmen laying over in the port, have troubled to come out in this awful weather just to jeer a minister caught on the other side in a downpour.

As a husband, father, and recent immigrant—by Edgartown standards at least—Uriah stands by his boat "overawed," the Reverend Vincent remembers.

He considers the mob, his two-cent fare, and perhaps his mortal soul; he decides that none of them is worth what might happen if he ferries Erastus over to town. With a last sorrowful look at the pastor, he turns away and trudges up to the house with his oars. "After waiting some time," Hebron recalls, "Mr. Otis had to wend his way back in the rain, to the nearest brother's, a mile distant."

More Sea Captains per Capita Than Anywhere Else

By the middle of the nineteenth century, more than forty men born and raised on Chappaquiddick are known to have become captains of sailing ships. It is reckoned that, per capita, this is more than any other place in the United States.

MARTHA'S VINEYARD CAMP-MEETING ASSOCIATION

Edgartown Methodists establish an annual summertime revival meeting in a forest near East Chop in 1835. Its fame soon spreads across the country.

But it is not long before Uriah achieves redemption.

His young daughter Mary attends a Methodist meeting in secret, finds salvation, and some days later approaches her father's workbench timidly. Uriah looks up.

"What does my child want?" he asks, and when Mary says she hopes to attend the Methodist meetings with his blessing, he looks at her a long moment and replies, "Yes. Go, child."

Moved by her request, he, too, converts "within the hour." Among other godly acts, he closes the dance hall and reopens it as the first official Methodist meeting-house in town. Thanks to him, never again will an evangelist have to wait for a Chappaquiddick ferryman on the Point and in the rain.

Uriah Morse dies on January 28, 1835, at the age of sixty-three. "He was a Christian man, lived beloved and died lamented," Hilda Allen of Edgartown remembers more than forty years later. "I have heard it said the procession that followed him to the cemetery was the largest ever formed on such an occasion before."

Ferry Schedule

- On call

Fare, 1811

- $.02 each way ($.26 in 2012 dollars)

Population on Chappaquiddick, 1797

- 190–200, among them 75 Wampanoags

CHAPTER 2

The Unnamed Ferryman

Circa 1835–1866

Uriah Morse rows his ferry into old age, perhaps up to the day he dies in late January 1835. With his death, history loses track of the Chappy ferry, to say nothing of the man—or men—who run it, for at least the next thirty years.

But at a hearing to license the ferry service at the start of the twentieth century, the owner claims to have proof the ferry has been in business, presumably without interruption, for the last one hundred years. And a thread of evidence suggests that through the end of the Civil War it remains a Morse family venture.

MARTHA'S VINEYARD MUSEUM

Captain John O. Morse

Uriah and Prudence Morse, who survives him by fifteen years, leave behind six adult children out of eight born to them. Uriah remains a waterfront laborer all his life, but he lives to see his oldest son become an aristocrat of the seas, among the most successful whaling masters that Edgartown ever produces.

Before he turns thirty, Captain John O. Morse, son of Uriah and Prudence, returns home in the New Bedford ship *Hector* with more than twenty-five hundred barrels of sperm oil, a remarkable haul of the most desirable product after a voyage of only two years and four months. On North Water Street, John builds a grand house with a front porch of two stories, pillared and crowned like a Greek temple.

North Water Street with Morse's Wharf in the background, circa 1887.

MARTHA'S VINEYARD MUSEUM

CHANTAL HODGES

Morse's Wharf with sail loft, early twentieth century.

In 1835 he is home between voyages, married and the father of the first of his seven children, when Uriah dies. Wanting to diversify his interests, John may—in a business sense—have been waiting for his father to go. Just forty-nine days after Uriah's death, John receives a permit from the state to build a commercial wharf, strategically closer to the busy harbor entrance than any other in town.

To build it, John probably tears down his own boyhood home, the house with the old dance hall on the main floor, as well as Uriah's coopering and boatbuilding shop below; records show that by 1850 the original Morse homestead on the waterfront is long gone, and his aging mother Prudence is living with a daughter and a son-in-law a block and a half inland.

On the wharf that John builds stands a large loft to make and repair sails, and to one side lies a new marine railway to haul and launch vessels from a new boatbuilding shop. This enterprise is called Morse's Wharf—today it is the site of the boatyard known as Edgartown Marine—and as befits the young patriarch of

CHANTAL HODGES

Steamer Uncatena *departs Edgartown after 1902.*

Steamers to the Mainland

Between 1834 and 1934, side-wheelers and propeller-driven steamships sail between Edgartown and the mainland carrying passengers and freight. When the county officially licenses the Chappy ferry in 1902, it stipulates that the ferryman must meet the arrival and departure of these steamers for the convenience of Chappy residents.

a rising family in a town growing rich on whaling voyages like John's, the road running along the length of his new mansion, down to his new wharf, is called Morse Street.

The road running along the length of John's new mansion, down to his new wharf, is called Morse Street.

John sets sail again before the end of 1835, and it is possible that as he departs Edgartown he hires his younger brother Stephen to serve as wharfinger, or manager, of Morse's Wharf; Stephen is known to be managing the wharf from at least the early 1850s until his death in 1866.

To attract patronage, Stephen perhaps takes up the ferry after his father dies and brother leaves. He may also share the duty with a younger brother, Uriah, a

MARTHA'S VINEYARD MUSEUM

Chappaquiddick Point, circa 1890–1910.

boatbuilder who uses the new marine railway next door. Or he may hire a skipper or lease the service to someone else. But there is every reason to believe the Chappy ferry remains a Morse family business through the Civil War.

It is the most profitably industrious time that Edgartown will ever know.

"I am informed that eighty captains of whaling ships belong to Edgartown," writes pastor Samuel Adams Devens in 1836. "They sail mostly from N. Bedford and are esteemed the most skillful and trust-worthy that can be found."

Among other holdings, Dr. Daniel Fisher of Edgartown runs the most successful oil and candle-making factory in the world. The time is not long past when the women of the seaport knit fifteen thousand pairs of stockings and three thousand mittens for visiting seamen every year. "It used to be said that when you reached Cape Poge Light," writes Samuel, "you could hear the knitting needles at Edgartown."

But in these palmy days, shadows begin to lengthen over the waterfront, and worrisome trends abound, even for ferrymen.

The middle of the nineteenth century is the most profitably industrious time Edgartown will ever know.

A Tide of Iniquity on Our Village Streets

V*ineyard Gazette* editorial, August 5, 1864: *Must the village of Edgartown, which has been noted for its quiet peacefulness, its correct morals, and its empty jail, be turned into a perfect Pandemonium by the boisterous conduct of a few lewd girls, rowdyish smackmen, and half grown boys, whose parents, if they have any, ought to be ashamed of their conduct?*

As we pen these lines our ears are nearly stunned with the hideous yells which come from the opposite side of the street. Our attention is so much disturbed that we open the door and find that they proceed from a score or more men in pursuit of a half dozen filthy, dirty, ragged women who are a disgrace to their sex and to humanity itself. . . .

MARTHA'S VINEYARD MUSEUM

Intersection of Main and Water streets, circa 1890. To right, North Water leads to the original Chappy ferry landing.

CONSTITUTION
OF THE
VINEYARD MINING COMPANY.

We, the undersigned, do agree to form ourselves into an Association, for the purpose of Mining in California, to be called the VINEYARD MINING COMPANY; and to secure the successful prosecution of the objects of this Company, we agree to adopt the following

RULES AND REGULATIONS:

Constitution of the Vineyard Mining Company, 1849, John O. Morse the first in the list of signatories. Captain Morse commands the bark that carries Vineyard prospectors to the California gold rush.

The saltworks built on Chappy Point by James Bunting closes down not long after his death in 1835, and the little island no longer hosts religious meetings in secret; in the thirty short years since the days of Erastus Otis and the rainstorm on the Point, the Methodists have converted just about everybody in town and made Methodism respectable. The monumental whaling church, built near the crest of Main Street in 1843, testifies to that.

On Chappy and across the Vineyard, parents age as young men—both white and among the Wampanoags who remain—go to sea or take their families to the mainland where they can find a trade besides fishing, farming, or whaling.

"Thus it is that family after family has left, and Martha's Vineyard has peopled and enriched all regions with her men and her wealth," frets the *Vineyard Gazette* in the first week of November 1849. "So it will ever be, while little or nothing of labor and production is carried on upon this soil. It will be thought a good place from which to go forth and make money,—but not a good place to stay, and employ, and keep, and enjoy it in. Like New Hampshire, its eulogy will be, that it is a fine region—*to emigrate from*."

It is taken as a resounding vote of no confidence in the prospects of Edgartown, even at the very height of whaling, that at least 117 of the 550 men between the ages of eighteen and fifty—more than 20 percent—sail for the California gold rush in 1849.

Hedging his own bets against the business that has made him wealthy, Captain John O. Morse forsakes what would be his sixth whaling voyage, buys a bark named *Sarah*, and sails a crew of Edgartown prospectors around Cape Horn to San Francisco. John falls ill on the voyage home and dies in Paita, Peru, on May 27, 1851. He is forty-eight and leaves a wife,

Mary, and seven children including a daughter, also named Mary, whom he never meets and who dies as a toddler just four months later.

Stephen Morse, married and the father of a dozen children, carries on as manager of Morse's Wharf, and perhaps as the Chappaquiddick ferryman, until he dies on October 1, 1866. Succeeding him as wharfinger and in time as ferrymaster is a retired whaling captain from Cape Cod with an eye for a shapely leg.

Ferry Schedule

- On call

Fare through circa 1866

- Unknown (if still $.02 each way, $.29 in 2012 dollars)

Population on Chappaquiddick, 1849

- About eighty-five Wampanoags and perhaps as many whites

MARTHA'S VINEYARD MUSEUM

Vineyard Haven Harbor, then called Holmes Hole Harbor, in the 1800s.

Traffic across Nantucket Sound

Before the opening of the Cape Cod Canal in 1914, Vineyard and Nantucket sounds serve as the great coastal throughway for most of the ships sailing commercially between Boston and New York and beyond. In 1853 the Shovelful Shoals Lightship, stationed between Chappaquiddick and Nantucket, records the passage of 655 full-rigged ships, 961 sloops, 2,390 brigs, and 14,089 schooners for a total of 18,095 vessels.

CHAPTER 3

Consider H. Fisher

Circa 1866–1883

He is the first Chappaquiddick ferryman for whom we have a portrait. Taken around 1860 it shows a solid, rather meaty-faced man with wavy hair gazing directly at the camera, his mouth downturned, jaw set, and graying beard pointing sharply to the fore. It is the face of a man who knows how to command a whaling bark the same way he knows how to breathe.

MARTHA'S VINEYARD MUSEUM

Captain Consider H. Fisher

Born the second of eleven children in 1809 to Abigail and James Fish, about whom little is known, Consider H. Fisher moves to Edgartown as a young man, and like other members of his family he changes his last name soon after he arrives—from Fish to Fisher, for reasons left unrecorded.

In all likelihood, Consider chooses Edgartown because he wants to captain a whaling ship, and in the early 1800s no other town its size supplies more masters to the trade across the New England coastline. He commands his first whaler, the bark *George Washington* of Falmouth, before he turns twenty-seven, and near the end of his career his schooner *Altamaha* brings in $13,500—about $312,000 today—a record catch for a voyage of only six months.

Whaleship *Splendid* at Osborn's Wharf, circa 1872.

MARTHA'S VINEYARD MUSEUM

It is the face of a man who knows how to command a whaling bark the same way he knows how to breathe.

It is a dismal era to run the ferry, as Edgartown lapses into a depression that empties its wharves and dulls the spirit of its inhabitants.

Retired from whaling in 1857, Consider has been married to Hannah R. Butler for nearly thirty years. She has sailed with him on at least one voyage; apparently they never have children. Consider is also close to the Morse family of Edgartown. Uriah, son of the first ferryman, is a neighbor living two doors down on Morse Street; he is also Consider's brother-in-law. Stephen, an older son of the first Uriah and manager of Morse's Wharf, invests with Consider in the *Altamaha* before Consider takes her out on his last two whaling trips.

When Stephen Morse dies in October 1866, Consider succeeds him as wharfinger at Morse's Wharf. Since he is rowing the Chappaquiddick ferry up to the time of his own death seventeen years later, Consider may take over the ferry at this point, too.

It is a dismal era to run the little business. Edgartown—still so prosperous, but worrying about the future just before the Civil War—soon after lapses into a depression that empties its wharves, dulls the spirit of its inhabitants, and eventually forces the town to trade an economy of production for a much more fitful and limited one of service to vacationers.

Trials of Storms and Cold

It's the side of the Chappy ferry service most visitors never see—days and nights when the boats furrow their way through fields of ice, when wintry gales blast across the wide-open decks, when the hulls rock heavily from side to side on their way across, and when the flat-faced bows pound into heaving seas and spray hisses and sizzles backward over cars and trucks.

In the face of a tempest, it's mostly up to the skippers to decide when it's safe to cross and when they must stop running. The main exception is when a tropical system threatens. In the hours ahead of hurricane, the Coast Guard may order most or even all the ports along the coastline to close and decree that, even in an emergency, no commercial vessel may leave a dock without official permission granted by phone to the owner.

Captains often say the toughest six-hour shifts are those when the temperature quivers just above freezing, the coldest rains fall, and a northeaster buffets the body and seeks out exposed skin to lash. On the most frigid days or nights, Charlie Ross suits up as if for a spacewalk—long johns, lined jeans or insulated coveralls, a T-shirt, shirt, sweatshirt, ski jacket or down coat, and the warmest hat and gloves he owns.

Peter Wells and Sally Snipes, the owners of the ferry today, provide the captains and deckhands with waterproof foul-weather jackets and overall pants. The coats are bright orange to help swiftly locate a skipper or crew member who falls overboard (it hasn't happened in the modern era). Some captains and deckhands accessorize creatively: One skipper has been known to wear a ski mask in a snowstorm, and deckhand Maddie LeCoq has worn an old pair of fur-lined bedroom slippers.

It looked funny, but "they were so comfortable and warm and fluffy!" she says. And on the coldest trips across, warm and fluffy is all that counts.

MARK ALAN LOVEWELL

Ferry On Time III *stuck in ice off Memorial Wharf, late 1980s.*

VINEYARD GAZETTE

Harbor entrance during Hurricane Carol, August 31, 1954.

For the village, an industrial and adventuresome way of life ends with a quintuple heart punch: Prospectors discover oil in Titusville, Pennsylvania, in 1859. Confederate raiders attack and burn northern whaling ships—including an Edgartown whaler—and the Union scuttles many others to blockade the entrances to Southern ports. In the fall of 1871 most of what remains of Edgartown's own small whaling fleet is crushed by ice while hunting above the Arctic Circle. In 1873 there is a financial panic, and following it a nationwide depression.

In the fall of 1871 most of what remains of Edgartown's own small whaling fleet is crushed by ice while hunting above the Arctic Circle.

And then there is the brand-new problem of Cottage City—today the town of Oak Bluffs.

Beginning in August 1835 the Methodists of Edgartown, hoping to rekindle the fiery founding spirit of their adopted faith from thirty years before, hold a weeklong camp meeting in a forest of oaks near East Chop—geographically still part of Edgartown but a wilderness far from the distractions of business and comforts of the village.

By 1870 Wesleyan Grove is the largest and most famous annual revival meeting in the country. Thousands travel by steamboat to witness the spectacle of exhorters, believers, and converts coming to God in what is now the Camp Ground of Oak

NANTUCKET HISTORICAL ASSOCIATION

Journal kept aboard Peru, *1850.*

A Fierce and Maybe Merciless Captain

As captain of the Nantucket bark *Peru* in February 1850, Consider Fisher tacks his vessel into a nighttime gale off the Chilean port of Talcahuano and chases four deserters. The men have stolen a boat and row twenty miles into a headwind and rainstorm to get away from him and whatever sort of ship he runs.

Consider wants his boat back, not the crewmen. In the end, he catches them. History does not record what happens to the deserters.

Bluffs. Cottage City—a brand-new village of hotels, boardwalks, bathing beaches, and amusements encircling the Camp Ground—houses and entertains visitors when they've had enough of all that evangelism.

About five miles to the south, boosters in Edgartown do everything they can to draw these summertime crowds down to the faltering old seaport. They lay a road along the great curve of a beach that stretches between the two towns and even build a narrow-gauge railway from one village to the other. But vacationers want to spend their time in the lively new seaside town, not the dying old one.

Professor Nathaniel S. Shaler, an eminent geologist, visits Edgartown in 1874 and writes of a town "far advanced in decay," its last whaling vessel lying on a railway "stripped of its rigging, looking more like an effigy of a living craft" than a ship that once sailed the globe. He surveys the proud homes built by whaling masters such as John O. Morse only thirty or forty years before and declares them relics of "a period of prosperity which has passed, never to return."

MARTHA'S VINEYARD MUSEUM

Derelict whaler at Osborn's Wharf.

But on the wilds of Chappaquiddick things are different. Although the outpost never enjoys the riches of Edgartown when times are flush, yet self-sufficient in nearly all things, neither does Chappaquiddick suffer when business turns bad.

MARTHA'S VINEYARD MUSEUM

MARTHA'S VINEYARD MUSEUM

Idle whaleboats and whaling casks on Osborn's Wharf.

To contradict "the impression that Chappaquiddick is a very lonely and deserted place," writes a correspondent to the *Vineyard Gazette*, readers should know of a gathering at the Chappy home of Matthew P. Norton on New Year's Day in 1878: "The many friends came at an early hour. The tables of cake and confectionery were abundantly displayed. After supper all joined in singing many pieces in a manner which did credit to the participants. Miss Phebie E. Norton played and sang 'Silver Threads among the Gold,' which was very prettily rendered."

Consider Fisher continues to row a skiff on call between Chappy Point and Morse's Wharf, now more often referred to as North Wharf after the deaths of John, Stephen, and the younger Uriah. Edgartown is filled with whaling masters like Consider—aging, land-bound, restless men with the "leonine look which comes from long habit of command," many of them "bronzed, with the deep, ingrained hue got only within the tropics which never fades again," writes Nathaniel Shaler.

Edgartown is filled with whaling masters like Consider—aging, land-bound, restless men with the "leonine look which comes from long habit of command."

From his post on North Wharf, he is called Uncle Consider now, and tough as things are, strangers occasionally show up at the ferry to visit friends on Chappaquiddick. A story circulates that an attractive young lady boards his skiff one windy day. The boat heads out, and she soon realizes they are off course and nearing the harbor light. Worried, she points this out to the ferryman, and peppery old Consider replies that if she does not cover her limbs, they will soon be sailing off Cape Pogue, since he is having a hard time concentrating.

Widowed two years and without heirs, Consider Fisher dies at the age of seventy-four on April 29, 1883, leaving no will and an estate worth $314. He owns a bit of furniture in a dwelling no longer in his name, a pew in the Old Whaling Church, a few skiffs he rents to summer visitors when they appear, and his rowboat ferry and a float to which he moors it on the Edgartown side, together appraised at $15.

Replacing him is the son of a whaling master who is an expert rigger, a leader of search parties when boats wreck and men go missing, the first man to receive a license to run the Chappaquiddick ferry, and the operator who will row and own it for thirty-seven years—longer than anyone before or since. These are each achievements in and of themselves.

What makes them more noteworthy is the fact that Charles B. Osborn, the man who accomplishes all of them, is blind.

Ferry Schedule

- On call

Fare through 1883

- Unknown (if $.03 each way, $.69 in 2012 dollars)

Population on Chappaquiddick, 1889

- Fifty, estimated

MARTHA'S VINEYARD MUSEUM

Coal schooners and side-wheeler *Monohansett* at Edgartown between 1870 and 1903.

Chappaquiddick School in Need of Repair

SIDNEY N. RIGGS

On March 9, 1883, the *Vineyard Gazette* notes that the one-room Chappaquiddick schoolhouse needs new sheathing and shingles and that *common decency requires a complete new set of benches, desks, and other furniture.*

"The residents on Chappaquiddic pay a considerable tax, rarely call for assistance from the poor fund, get next to nothing for roads, and should at least be provided with reasonable school privileges and respectable schoolhouse appointments."

ON TIME III
FERRY
CAUTION
CROSSING
ON TIME III
EDGARTOWN

CHAPTER 4

Charles B. and Walstein Osborn

1883–1920

Ninety years later, it remains the obvious and lasting question to do with the long history of the Chappy ferry: How on earth does he manage it? How does Charles B. Osborn row a ferry for nearly four decades between Edgartown and Chappaquiddick when he cannot see?

How does Charles B. Osborn row a ferry for nearly four decades between Edgartown and Chappaquiddick when he cannot see?

Charlie Osborn is fourteen years old when cataracts begin to cloud his view of the world. He is an Edgartown boy, born August 27, 1859, the third of four children and only son of Achsah and James Coffin Osborn, a whaling captain. As his vision fails they take him to Boston, where doctors say they can do nothing, and for a time his parents grieve with him when it becomes plain that Charlie will never go whaling himself.

It is just about the only thing on the water he doesn't spend a lifetime doing.

As a young man he fishes from a boat and sails on schooners carrying freight up and down the New England coastline until the day comes when he no longer safely

W. H. Mayhew hardware store, a gathering place on North Water Street, circa 1899.

Suddenly a Boom on Chappaquiddick

Fed up with attempts to draw away her summer visitors, Cottage City—today Oak Bluffs—separates from Edgartown and incorporates as an independent town in 1880. Deprived of tax revenue from the prosperous satellite village, Edgartown—its whaling industry gone and hard times holding back its development as a resort—faces ruin. Wharves rot from disuse. Houses stand dark and empty all year long. The town is clearly dying.

But in the winter of 1889 three New York "gentlemen of means and leisure" visit Edgartown, and while there they cross the harbor and tour Chappaquiddick. From the hilltops, they take in a wilderness of scrub and farmland spreading outward toward a glittering harbor, pond, sound, and sea. By summer the first country homes on Chappy rise on the bluffs looking out over Katama Bay.

The building of these few villas touches off a land boom on Chappy. Longtime residents and landholders swiftly chop up the hills and plains into lots of fifty-by-a-hundred feet, give them dreamy names (the Region of Perfect Content at Wasque Point), and offer them for prices as low as fifteen dollars each. Promoters promise golf courses, hotels, yacht clubs, and direct and daily service by steamboat to the little island—exotic Cottage City attractions at introductory Chappaquiddick prices.

For a year or two, Edgartown feels flush. But then mainland buyers of the little lots actually visit Chappaquiddick and see not a resort but backcountry and nothing but a rowboat ferry to get them there. Most never return. The boom ends as quickly as it begins.

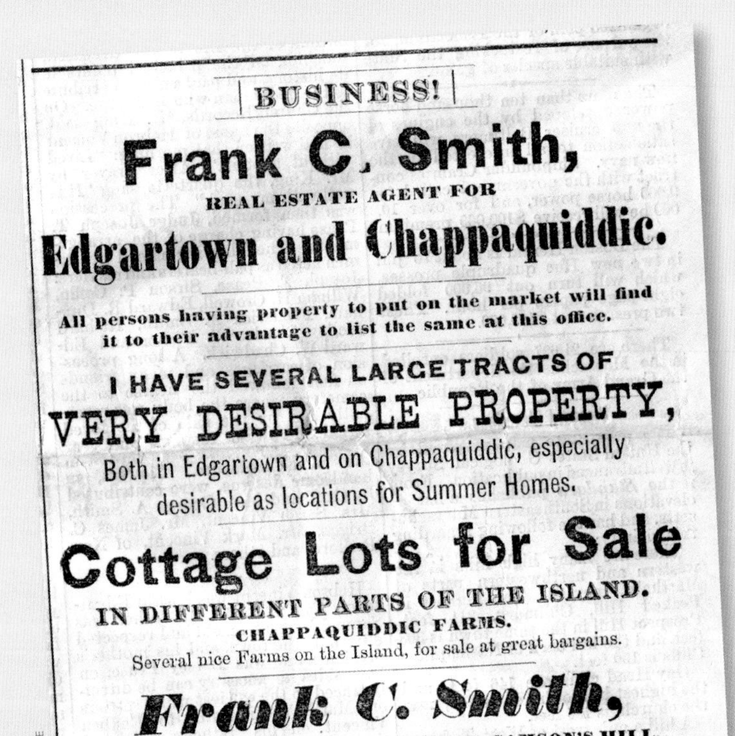
BUSINESS!

Frank C. Smith,

REAL ESTATE AGENT FOR

Edgartown and Chappaquiddic.

All persons having property to put on the market will find it to their advantage to list the same at this office.

I HAVE SEVERAL LARGE TRACTS OF

VERY DESIRABLE PROPERTY,

Both in Edgartown and on Chappaquiddic, especially desirable as locations for Summer Homes.

Cottage Lots for Sale

IN DIFFERENT PARTS OF THE ISLAND.

CHAPPAQUIDDIC FARMS.

Several nice Farms on the Island, for sale at great bargains.

Frank C. Smith,

HUXFORD VILLA, - - NEAR SAMSON'S HILL,

Chappaquiddic, Edgartown, Mass.

VINEYARD GAZETTE

Advertisement during the Chappy land boom, 1890.

MARTHA'S VINEYARD MUSEUM

Charlie Osborn, with bass drum, and the Edgartown Cornet Band at town hall, 1902.

can. Ashore he learns the craft of rigging, a trade requiring a wrestler's strength and a seamstress's touch. After a great sailing vessel arrives in Edgartown, Charlie and others disassemble, repair, or replace everything above the main deck—sails, ropes, stays, and spars—and re-rig the vessel before she sails again.

He works in a loft above what is now the Edgartown Yacht Club. The floor and much of the tackle is thick with tar, and Charlie soaks his hands in grease each morning to keep his fingers separate and nimble. The room is dark, and what's left of his smeary vision does him little good while he works.

Ashore Charlie Osborn learns the craft of rigging, a trade requiring a wrestler's strength and a seamstress's touch.

The hempen stays that support the mast of a sailing ship measure as much as four inches around. Charlie pries apart the strands, runs heavy marlin through them with a thick needle, wraps them in canvas, and secures them with lighter marlin and a special mallet. By feel he learns all the knots and splices of the art, as well as how to mend heavy wooden spars and canvas sails—always mindful that the lives of the crew and safety of the ship and cargo depend on the work he does. He knows, too, that no captain will ever accept his blindness as an excuse when he inspects Charlie's handiwork.

JERRY GRANT

Charlie Osborn's ferryhouse, circa 1895–1899.

He takes over the Chappaquiddick ferry on the death of Consider Fisher in May 1883. Under Charlie, the Edgartown ferry landing moves a few feet south of North Wharf. On this neighboring lot, Charlie owns a tumbledown shack of a ferryhouse, and from a spindly pier, angling toward Chappy Point, he rows his ferry and rents a small fleet of rowboats and catboats to the few summer visitors who are, at last, giving the relic seaport of Edgartown a curious look. He also teaches people to sail.

Which begs the question: Just how bad is Charlie Osborn's eyesight?

Newspaper stories about Charlie in his prime never mention his blindness, and in old age a young friend writes that sightlessness is "one part of him that he was always very sensitive about; he hated others to speak of it, and disliked to mention it himself."

As an older man, Charlie can feel his way around a cribbage board, and if he holds it up to his face, he can make out the rank and suit of a playing card. But beyond this, the world is a gauzy place. "One often sees him groping along the pier with a shuffling, hesitating gait," writes the friend, "his hands outstretched to prevent his bumping into obstructions."

"One often sees him groping along the pier with a shuffling, hesitating gait, his hands outstretched to prevent his bumping into obstructions."

If his vision is anywhere near this poor when he is younger, then Charlie must know Edgartown Harbor more subtly and deeply than any other man of his day. Rowing from the ferry landing on either side, he feels the current and breeze act

View down to North Wharf, after 1899. Osborn ferryhouse is the second building on the right.

MARTHA'S VINEYARD MUSEUM

MARTHA'S VINEYARD MUSEUM

Casemiro Bettencourt commands the Chappy-by-the-Sea *launch.*

Chappaquiddick-by-the-Sea Launch

In 1913, developers plot out of 750 houses called Chappaquiddick-by-the-Sea on the southeastern corner of the island. To encourage buyers, they run a double-ended launch from what is now the Edgartown Yacht Club wharf to a pier at the far end of Katama Bay. The captain of the launch is Casemiro Bettencourt, father of a future captain of the Chappaquiddick ferry. Only three houses are ever built at the development. A large part of it now belongs to the Wasque preserve of the Trustees of the Reservations, a land conservation group. The launch stops running after the 1914 summer season.

on his skiff, senses shifts in temperature and brightness as one shoreline recedes and the other approaches, and smells seaweed on the beach as he nears Chappy Point or scallop shells on the bulkhead as he nears his ferryhouse.

In the harbor, Edgartown men skippering small boats know Charlie well and regard his blindness as a fact of life, steering around him as they would anyone else in a rowboat. As for larger vessels, Charlie can surely tell the distance, angle, and speed of an advancing schooner or bark by the rhythm of her bow wave or the slatting of her canvas as she tacks—enough to know when to row and when to stop. If he has a passenger he might receive a word of counsel if he asks.

This leaves out the whole matter of his strength and skill at the oars. Through much of the first half of his ownership of the ferry, South Beach is open to the sea, so the tides running through the harbor are powerful and capricious. Yet when people want to cross with a cart, wagon, and horse or oxen, Charlie simply lays planks across his wide, flat-bottomed boat and rows with the wagon balanced above him, his passenger holding a lead from the stern as the animals swim behind.

Indeed, it soon becomes plain that the only thing the ferry cannot do under the captaincy of Charlie Osborn is keep up with transformational times. During his tenure the first car sails over to Chappaquiddick, visitors build the first summer homes there, and a competitor first challenges the Chappy ferry. It may be said that

Indeed, it soon becomes plain that the only thing the ferry cannot do under the captaincy of Charlie Osborn is keep up with transformational times.

MARTHA'S VINEYARD MUSEUM

Bathing beach at Chappaquiddick, now the Chappy Beach Club, in the 1890s.

At a hearing called December 11, 1902, by the county commissioners, the Edgartown selectmen acknowledge the necessity of a year-round ferry but declare themselves reluctant to subsidize it.

modernity comes to Chappy during the ownership of Charles Osborn, and each advance leaves him, his ferry, and his disability just a little further behind.

The first test comes from an Edgartown businessman named Edward Chadwick and his sons, James and Harlan. In 1883, the same year Charlie takes over the ferry, the Chadwicks establish a public bathing beach on the long crescent of Chappaquiddick Point facing the outer harbor, where the Chappy Beach Club stands today. The bathing beach starts off with three bathhouses; by 1899 there are nearly two hundred. That summer James Chadwick buys a thirty-seven-foot steam launch called *Ah-There* and renames it *Irene* after a daughter.

Walstein Osborn

When Walstein Osborn isn't rowing the ferry late in his father's career, he travels from house to house in Edgartown, beating rugs and selling the kindling he collects from the beach after storms. Known to his family as Wally and to Chappy and the town as Steen, he wears thick glasses, the lenses frosted at the sides to help him focus. He lives alone after the deaths of his father in 1946 and mother Blanche Galley Osborn in 1958 and dies on January 12, 1961. He is buried with his parents at the Westside Cemetery in Edgartown.

A canopy shading her beachgoing passengers, the *Irene* steams smoothly between the Chappy bathing beach and two Edgartown piers owned by the Chadwick family—one of them North Wharf, right next door to Charlie's boathouse and little rowboat ferry. Charlie's summertime revenues plummet. At the end of the season the Chadwicks decommission the *Irene*, leaving Charlie with the burden of a winter service that often earns him less than a dollar a week.

The first great crisis in the hundred-year history of the Chappy ferry begins when Charlie suspends service in the fall of 1902 to work at other jobs. No longer a frontier at the turn of the twentieth century, Chappaquiddick finds itself surprisingly and uncomfortably dependent on Edgartown—and the ferry—in all sorts of vital ways.

Her daughter seriously ill, Mrs. Marshall Mead of Chappaquiddick hurries to the Point one day that autumn and rings the bell for the ferry. But Charlie does not come. On three occasions, the Chappaquiddick teacher comes down to the Point at the end of the school day and rings the bell. But Charlie does not come. Physicians, handymen, friends of Island residents—all sorts of people who, in earlier times, might be counted on to have boats of their own now find themselves stranded on one side or another simply because the weather turns cold, the summer visitors leave, and the ferry no longer comes.

Under state law, the county licenses and regulates ferries at its discretion. At a hearing called December 11, 1902, by the county commissioners, the Edgartown selectmen acknowledge the necessity of a year-round ferry but declare themselves reluctant to subsidize it. After all, the town does not pay for a fire department on Chappy, nor police, nor water, nor road maintenance, nor repair of the schoolhouse, nor much of anything else—and it never has. Why support a ferry that earns less than a dollar a week on its own?

Yet necessity carries the day. That week, the county commissioners license the

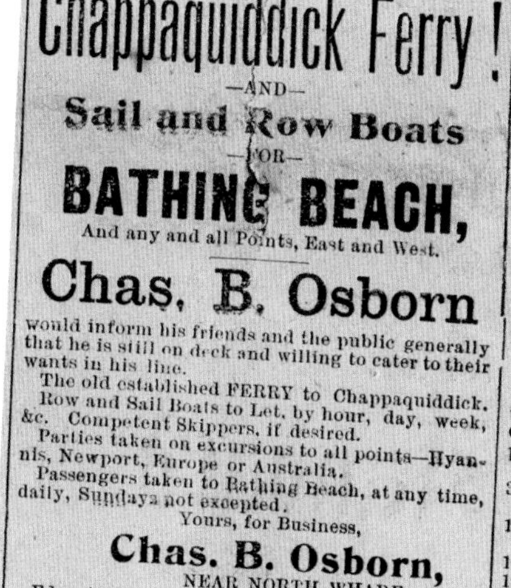

Chappaquiddick Ferry!

—AND—

Sail and Row Boats

—FOR—

BATHING BEACH,

And any and all Points, East and West.

Chas. B. Osborn

would inform his friends and the public generally that he is still on deck and willing to cater to their wants in his line.

The old established FERRY to Chappaquiddick.

Row and Sail Boats to Let, by hour, day, week, &c. Competent Skippers, if desired.

Parties taken on excursions to all points—Hyannis, Newport, Europe or Australia.

Passengers taken to Bathing Beach, at any time, daily, Sundays not excepted.

Yours, for Business,

Chas. B. Osborn,
NEAR NORTH WHARF.

Edgartown, Aug. 10, 1899.

[From Salem Evening News, Aug. 5th.]

MR. HUSSEY GOES ABROAD.

William Penn Hussey, the financier and coal baron whose name has become famous on two continents during past few years, sailed from New York on the S. S. Umbria of the Cunard line for England, this morning, in response to a cable from leading capitalists of that country and of the eastern continent, for an immediate personal interview concerning a deal in con-

STEAMER "AH-THERE"

—FOR—

Chappaquiddick Bathing Beach

—LEAVES—

North Wharf,

Chadwick's Wharf,

Collins' Wharf.

Until further notice, wind and weather permitting, the 40-foot passenger steamer "Ah-There," Capt. R. D. Smith, will ply between the above points as follows Sundays excepted:

LEAVE COLLINS' WHARF, at 9.52 a. m , 2.52, 3.22, 3.52 and 4.22 p. m.

LEAVE CHADWICK'S WHARF, at 9.55, 10.55 and 11.55 a. m., 2.55, 3 25, 3.55 and 4.25 p. m.

LEAVE NORTH WHARF, foot of Morse street, at 10.00, 10.15, 10.30, 10 45, 11.00, 11.15, 11.30, 11.45 a. m., 12.00 m., 12.15, 12 30 and 12.45 p. m , for Bathing Beach. RETURN, leave Beach 5 minutes later on above times.

IN AFTERNOONS steamer will leave North Wharf every 30 minutes from 3 until 4 30 o'clock. Leave Beach, last trip, at 5 p. m.

☞The 1 p. m. Return trip goes to Collins' Wharf.

☞The 10.35, 11.35 a. m., and 12.35 p. m Return trips go to Chadwick's Wharf.

☞All Return trips stop at North Wharf.

Steamer can be chartered for excursions, day or evening, outside of Bathing hours above named.

H. C. CHADWICK, Proprietor.

Edgartown, July 26, 1899.

VINEYARD GAZETTE

Dueling ferry ads, summer of 1899.

First Streetlamp on Chappy

Vineyard Gazette, August 6, 1903: *The march of progress goes constantly forward, and now Chappaquiddick takes on metropolitan trimmings. The first street lamp ever erected on that beautiful isle has recently been placed in position near 'Look-out Cottage,' and its beams nightly illume the way to the Chadwick summer residence on the hill.*

Chappy ferry for the first time, stipulating that Charlie must run all year, meet the mainland steamers that sail to and from what is now Memorial Wharf, and charge no more than a nickel per passenger. The town agrees to subsidize the service to the tune of a dollar a day. But the commissioners cannot prohibit or regulate the competition, and inevitably the *Irene* returns the following season, a summertime launch outdrawing the year-round rowboat by hundreds, perhaps even thousands, to one.

And there can be no question about the suburbanizing influences at work on Chappaquiddick as of the afternoon of Thursday, July 18, 1912:

"We understand the first automobile on the island of Chappaquiddick went careering over hill and dale yesterday afternoon," reports the *Vineyard Gazette*. "It was taken over on a large scow

VINEYARD GAZETTE

Ho! for Chappaquiddick!

If you want to go to any part of Chappaquiddick at any hour Handy is the man to take you there. Two and Three-Seaters for passengers and baggage and freight wagons. Telegrams delivered and care taken with all sorts of commissions. Great season promised for beach plums and huckleberries—Handy will take your party to the best pickings. If you want anything in connection with Earth's Most Beautiful Island, get into touch with Handy —he will do the rest. Leave orders at store of Thomas Mellen or at Osborn's Ferry House, or drop a postal direct to WM. H. HANDY, (Chappaquiddick,) Edgartown, Mass.

Above: Ad for William Handy, Chappy jack-of-all-trades, summer 1905.

MARTHA'S VINEYARD MUSEUM

Right: North Water Street in a new era, summer of 1918.

MARTHA'S VINEYARD MUSEUM

Charlie Osborn at his Edgartown landing with four passengers, circa 1895.

and belongs to Dr. Frank L. Marshall of Boston, who has a summer place near Joel's Landing. We are told the frequent honks as it proceeded to the Doctor's place so aroused some of the staid inhabitants that Gov. Handy"—William Handy, a Chappy factotum and deliveryman—"came to town to see what it was all about."

Whatever way the car and barge manage to sail over to Chappy, it is evident that Charlie Osborn is not in charge. He spends his lifetime skippering a rowboat, but plainly a blind man cannot command a motorboat towing a scow and automobile. Though cars cross to Chappy only occasionally in the next ten years, Charlie understands the ferry service is moving beyond him, and he shifts his attention to his growing fleet of rental boats. More and more he turns over the rowing of the Chappy ferry to his son Walstein, nearly blind himself and, in the language of the day, "slow."

Charlie finally resigns the ferry service in January or early February 1920. With the one-room Chappy schoolhouse closed since 1916, islanders learn of Charlie's departure only after their children go to the Point several days in a row and—once again—no one appears to ferry them to the town and school.

"Many are wondering why the School children of Chappaquiddick are being deprived of their education which in most cases their parents are paying for in taxation," writes Leroy W. Vose of Edgartown. "In-as-much as Mr. Osborn has resigned, it would seem that someone might want the position which certainly is capable of making a good living for the right person."

Charlie Osborn's successor turns out to be a stout man with powerful arms and a sense of humor about himself and his service. But the sort of ferry he runs makes Chappaquiddickers want desperately to build a bridge.

Ferry Schedule

- 1883–1902: On call
- 1902–1920: Ferry to meet all arriving and departing mainland steamships between 6:00 a.m. and 7:00 p.m.
- Ferryman also in attendance: 8:00 a.m.–noon, 1:00 p.m.–4:00 p.m., and 5:00 p.m.–7:00 p.m.

Fares, 1902–1920

- Passenger: $.05 each way (1902 fare is $1.24 in 2012 dollars)
- Trunk: $.15 each (1902 fare is $3.73 in 2012 dollars)
- $1.00 daily subsidy by town (1902 subsidy is $24.86 in 2012 dollars)

Population on Chappaquiddick, 1889

- Fifty estimated, year-round

CHAPTER 5

James H. Yates
1920–1929

Folks on both sides of the harbor love Jimmy Yates. But folks on the Chappaquiddick side loathe the ferry Jimmy Yates runs.

James H. Yates is born in Edgartown on July 10, 1876, the son of James S. Yates of the village and Marietta Fisher Yates of Nantucket. Jimmy works in a parade of jobs as a young man on the Vineyard and mainland—grocery clerk, deliveryman, assistant plumber, shoe salesman—but after the Spanish-American War he moves to Cuttyhunk, outermost in a chain of islands on the far side of Vineyard Sound, where he fishes and salvages wrecks with his father-in-law.

Jimmy returns to Edgartown with a daughter and his wife, Mabel, who dies in 1915 at the age of thirty-one. He takes over the ferry on the retirement of Charlie and Walstein Osborn in 1920, and for the second time on the Edgartown side, the service moves, from the Osborn boathouse a hundred yards south to a weedy beach just north of the steamboat wharf, the site of the ferry landing today.

It is a startling fact of history—and for Chappaquiddickers, a profoundly frustrating one—that until the day Jimmy Yates retires in the spring of 1929, the Chappy ferry remains a rowboat service.

VINEYARD GAZETTE

Captain James H. Yates, 1925.

Until the day Jimmy Yates retires in the spring of 1929, the Chappy ferry remains a rowboat service.

CHANTAL HODGES

Postcard of Edgartown Harbor at the turn of the twentieth century.

The paper calls him Commodore Yates, and summer residents on the Edgartown side, joining in the merriment, present him a blue yachting cap embellished with gold braid and a silver badge.

Throughout the decade, Chappy residents look across the channel to Edgartown and see the equivalent of Paris—a village of electric lights, telephones, paved roads, and drivers of automobiles going wherever they want, whenever they want. Chappy has none of these things, and islanders reckon they never will so long as they let the town get away with subsidizing a rowboat ferry in a Henry Ford age.

In the course of his ownership, Jimmy seldom rows more than two or three people an hour even in summer, which may be why he never shows any interest in bringing the operation into the motorboat and car ferry era. Instead, with *Pinafore*-like grandeur, he plays up the ironies of his antiquated command, costuming himself in a serge vest with brass buttons, watch chain, and sunflower in his lapel—all this for a service that sails just 527 feet from point to Point.

The paper calls him Commodore Yates, and summer residents on the Edgartown side, joining in the merriment, present him a blue yachting cap embellished with gold braid and a silver badge. "On it is inscribed, 'Edgartown Ferryman 241,'" reports the *Vineyard Gazette*. "Just why this mystic number was chosen is a matter for debate but the most popular interpretation is that those who contributed toward the purchase are planning to get two rides for one."

Jimmy's ferryhouse faces Dock Street, and next door stands the boatbuilding shop of Manuel Swartz Roberts, now the Old Sculpin Gallery.

Between fares, Jimmy loiters with the Edgartown men who visit Manuel every day. It is a town of pranksters, and Jimmy's rowboat, beached not seventy-five feet away, is the ripest of waterfront targets. One afternoon, Jimmy hears the bell on the Chappy side and sets off from the beach. A few dozen feet from shore, the skiff halts sharply, and no matter how hard Jimmy rows, he can go no farther; Manuel and the boys have tied a swordfishing line from a wharf to an eyebolt below the waterline of his boat.

MARTHA'S VINEYARD MUSEUM

Yates ferry, lettered by pranksters, 1924.

On Chappaquiddick, however, Jimmy Yates's ferry is no joke at all, and as visitors begin to rent houses for the summer in Edgartown, Chappy lags because there is no easy way to go back and forth. On the night of February 28, 1924, island residents take to the floor of the town meeting to propose a way around the whole ferry problem. It will cost no more

Edgartown's Master Boatbuilder

When the shop of Manuel Swartz Roberts closes in 1954 after half a century of boatbuilding, one village resident declares it to be "the biggest upheaval this town has ever known."

Rising just a few steps from the Edgartown ferry slip, Manuel's shop is a daily stop "for every thinking man in town," recalls S. Bailey Norton, who knows him from his boyhood in the 1920s.

Manuel serves as host and impromptu philosopher to his friends, stepping aside to solve problems, settle disputes, and even visit homes to quiet the spirits of restive ghosts. He repairs toys for youngsters and chairs for housewives, using tools so ancient he cannot guess their age and others he designs and tempers himself.

The models of two of Manuel's catboats are now archived at the Smithsonian Museum. Most measuring no longer than twenty-four feet, and all of them working under sail, his catboats fish as far offshore as the trans-Atlantic shipping lanes and withstand every imaginable storm and sea.

He builds launches, too, and rowboats, and sloops in which summer children learn to sail and race. Over the course of twenty-one years, between 1927 and 1948, he also builds, rebuilds, or helps to build seven boats that serve as Chappy ferries or launches to the bathing beach.

Manuel's shop today serves as the gallery of the Martha's Vineyard Art Association. It borrows the nickname bestowed upon him years before: the Old Sculpin, a bony fish with a large head, which roughly traces the physique of Edgartown's master boatbuilder.

Today, in a gallery often hung with paintings of an Edgartown waterfront his artistry and labors helped preserve, visitors can feel a swale in the planking, worn there by Manuel as he walked back and forth along his workbench for nearly half a century.

SALLY SANIUTA

Manuel Swartz Roberts in his boatbuilding shop, now the Old Sculpin Gallery, late in his career.

ROY MEEKINS

On the waterfront: Roberts boatbuilding shop far right, Yates ferryhouse three buildings to the left.

Yes, the ferry is "rotten," concedes Benjamin G. Collins, a town selectman, but the village carries too much debt to build a bridge.

than one hundred thousand dollars to build, last four hundred years, require just two hundred dollars annually to maintain, and be paid for by an immediate rise in the value of land on Chappy and the tax revenue that this rise will generate.

What Chappy wants is a bridge.

It need not be elaborate, say those who think it up; a footbridge would do at first. As designed by the American Bridge Company of New York City, it looks like a railroad trestle in three spans, each measuring 208 feet, rising no more than 50 feet above the harbor, and crossing at the narrows where colonial farmers once swam their cattle to graze on Chappaquiddick.

But the proposal leaves out the crucial facts that, as designed, the bridge will land on a private waterfront estate in Edgartown as much as a quarter of a mile from the main road on Chappaquiddick; that once on the Edgartown side, those who use it will still face a mile-long walk into town; and that 50 feet is too low for the masts of the largest sailboats to clear as they sail to and from Katama Bay. It takes a year, but at the next town meeting, Edgartown voters turn down the bridge idea, 99-58.

Chappaquiddick quickly raises the stakes. Six months later, in August 1925, all sixteen voters on the island, together with thirteen other landholders, file a petition with the state to separate from Edgartown and incorporate as the town of Chappaquiddick.

Chappy has one asset that it can hold hostage as Edgartown considers a response: access to the valuable shellfishing grounds at Cape Pogue Pond. Edgartown brushes aside the threat: At the next town meeting—which Chappaquiddickers boycott—the town votes symbolically 108-1 against Chappy independence. It also votes to hire a lawyer to protect its interests.

On the rainy afternoon of April 8, 1926, members of the state legislative committee on towns visit Chappaquiddick to determine whether it should be allowed to go its own way. Jimmy Yates rows the committeemen over to the Point for a tour, and at least one problem to do with the ferry presents itself when Representative Josiah Babcock of Milton, believing the skiff has landed on the beach, steps over the side and into water up to his waist.

Three hundred citizens attend a committee hearing held that night at town hall. Benjamin W. Pease of Chappy testifies that fifty-three people have left the island in his lifetime because of the poor ferry and refusal of Edgartown to meet basic island needs. When his father died one winter, Ben says, Edgartown charged his mother one hundred dollars to clear the road of snow so that the body could be brought to town for burial.

Yes, the ferry is "rotten," concedes Benjamin G. Collins, a town selectman, but the village carries too much debt to build a bridge. There is already a motorized launch to the bathing beach in summer, he adds. And most Chappaquiddickers have their own boats anyway. "If it wasn't for the $100,000 yearly shellfish catch, the grounds of which are mostly in Chappaquiddick waters," he declares, "I would say, 'Go and God bless you.'"

Above: Ferry *On Time III* approaches marine railway in Vineyard Haven for a refit, fall of 2011.

Below: Profile of the Chappy bridge, 1924.

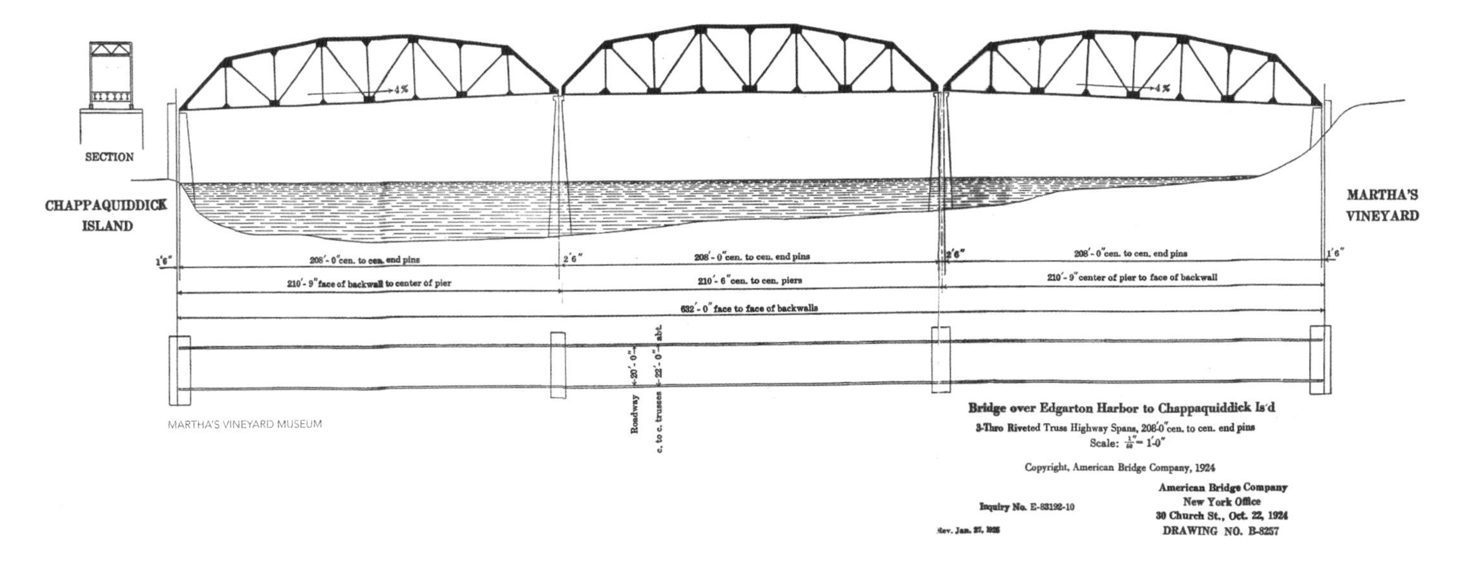

MARTHA'S VINEYARD MUSEUM

In February 1927, the town meeting commissions Manuel Swartz Roberts to build the first town-sponsored boat for the Chappaquiddick ferry.

It's not known whether Jimmy Yates attends the meeting or how he responds to hearing his ferry characterized as "rotten"—other descriptions include "hazard" and "disgrace"—but it is no surprise when the committee refuses to endorse the creation of a new town of just sixteen voters. Yet legislators depart Edgartown with the pointed remark that they know "no parallel in Massachusetts of an island dependency effectively cut off from its parent town."

Edgartown takes the cue—if it ever wants anything from the state again, it had better do something about this problem soon—and in February 1927 the town meeting commissions Manuel Swartz Roberts, the village boatbuilder, to build the first town-sponsored boat for the Chappaquiddick ferry. But the new boat is nothing more than a $250 barge, designed to carry a single car, and no provision is made to build or buy a powerboat to tow it.

No Immodesty When It Comes to Swimwear

James Chadwick, proprietor of the bathing beach at Chappaquiddick, is a strict Methodist, and through the 1920s he tolerates no immodesty when it comes to swimwear. "These Rules Will Be Rigidly Enforced" declares a sign at the beach: "1) Bare-legged women will not be tolerated. 2) Women bathers must wear stockings—not sox. 3) One-piece bathing suits are forbidden, both for men and women. 4) Skirts (bathing suit) must come to the knees. 5) Coming to beach in bathing suits is forbidden."

Bathing beach on Chappaquiddick, 1937.

TILGHMAN FAMILY

Thus it becomes one of the wonders of the age to see Jimmy Yates, at sixty-one, pulling the barge loaded down with a Model A across the entrance to the harbor. Together, car and scow can weigh nothing less than two tons. Yet the challenge is one not just of weight, but also of current. In 1921 the town digs a new cut through South Beach—an opening created by a storm in 1886 having closed naturally in 1903—in the belief that the shellfishing beds in Katama Bay do better when the harbor is connected directly to the sea.

As a result, the tides once again funnel through the harbor entrance forcefully, and Jimmy must wait for those rare moments when the currents slacken just long enough to pull across the barge and car. On occasion he finds another man to help haul from a second boat. But not often. "Years of pulling at the oars made the ferryman's arms tremendously powerful," says the *Gazette* after his death in January 1942.

The most mysterious thing about the tenure of Jimmy Yates is what happens at the very end of it. In the spring of 1929 the town finally builds a power launch to tow the barge and cars—at a cost of $2,015, with Manuel again the builder.

But as the new motorboat goes in the water, Jimmy quits. A nineteenth-century man to the last day of his service, he apparently wants nothing to do with the sort of traffic a mechanized operation will surely bring. With his yachting cap, badge, and sunflower boutonniere, Jimmy Yates and a rowboat era lasting more than 125 years depart the annals of the Chappaquiddick ferry.

Replacing him as ferryman is a boyhood immigrant from the Azores, short of stature and visionary in thought and deed.

Ferry Schedule, 1920–1929

- Likely the same as his predecessor, Charles Osborn: Ferry to meet all arriving and departing mainland steamships between 6:00 a.m. and 7:00 p.m.
- Ferryman also in attendance between 8:00 a.m. and noon, 1:00 p.m.–4:00 p.m., and 5:00 p.m.–7:00 p.m.

Fares, 1920–1929

- Passenger: $.06 each way (1920 fare is $.79 in 2012 dollars)
- Car and driver: $.50 each way in 1929 (1920 fare is $6.61 in 2012 dollars)
- $1.00 daily subsidy by town (1920 subsidy is $13.23 in 2012 dollars)

Population on Chappaquiddick, 1924

- Twenty-five estimated, year-round

PAINTING BY PATRICIA MEAD

OPEN

CHAPTER 6

Anthony A. Bettencourt

1929–1948

Little in the background of Anthony A. Bettencourt suggests he will be the fellow who reinvents the Chappaquiddick ferry. While townspeople bestow three nicknames upon him besides Tony—Midge, Midgie, or Tony Midge because he stands about five feet five—on Chappy the service he runs for nineteen years is known by only one: Tony's Ferry.

He is born on Graciosa, one of the smaller islands in the central Azores, at a half-hour before midnight on December 31, 1899. His parents, Casemiro (Casemede) and Mary Medina Bettencourt, immigrate to New England when Tony is one, and they settle first in Edgartown and then on Chappy in 1903.

He leaves the Chappaquiddick School when he is thirteen, replacing his father as captain of a thirty-foot launch for Mr. and Mrs. Horace W. Gridley, summer pioneers on Chappy during the land boom beginning in 1889. It is Tony's first job ferrying people back and forth to Edgartown. Loyal, hardworking, and sunny, he works for the Gridleys for the next fifteen years and is serving as the family chauffeur when he departs to take over the ferry from Jimmy Yates on May 3, 1929.

BETTENCOURT FAMILY

Tony Bettencourt in his new passenger launch, 1929.

That week the operation leaves behind the rowboat era, evolving at last into a service with a powerboat. Paid for by the town and designed and built by Manuel Swartz Roberts, the first motorized ferry is a twenty-foot launch, carrying passengers when there are no cars and towing the barge when there are. With construction of this launch, the town stops paying the ferrymaster his dollar-a-day subsidy. Financially the service and its owner are once again entirely on their own.

On Chappaquiddick, the ferry service he runs for nineteen years is known by only one name: Tony's Ferry.

The new launch goes into the water without a christening or a name and never gets one. Passengers find the vessel swift and comfortable after traveling for a century and a quarter in a rowboat. But Tony—drawing on his long experience driving the Gridley limousine back and forth to Edgartown—sees right away that a launch towing a barge and car is almost as awkward as a rowboat towing a barge and car.

The skipper, for example, must tie the barge alongside the launch because it swings off course in the current if towed from astern. Also, there are no slips in which to dock the barge; the ferryman noses it up to the beach, lays two planks ten inches wide from the sand up to the deck, and coaxes a car aboard. And the barge can carry only one car at a time, and barely a limo of Gridleyesque length.

There must be a better way, but it requires thinking entirely anew.

"Around 1934 I had an idea that a motor raft would run perfectly if you rigged it up like a boat," Tony recalls thirty years later. What he envisions looks like the existing barge, except it will be ten feet longer and a little wider so that it can carry two cars and a few passengers as well. What makes it revolutionary is the fact that it will have its own engine, creating—in effect—a barge without a tug, one that the ferryman can drive and steer all on its own.

"Manuel kind of discouraged me," says Tony, "but he set to work building a scow with a skeg on it." The skeg, a shallow keel running along the flat of the bottom, is a critical part of the new design; without one, the scow would slide sideways with the current even as she propels herself forward. The skeg will solve another problem: what to run the propeller shaft through and hang the rudder from. A prop and rudder also mean the town must build slips on both sides, because beach landings in shallow water would damage them both.

The ferry Tony envisions looks like the existing barge, but what makes it revolutionary is that it will have its own engine, propeller, and helm—a barge that the ferryman can drive and steer all on its own.

Passenger launch and barge at the present-day Edgartown ferry slip, circa 1929–1934.

CHANTAL HODGES

A Conflagration in the Night

Tony's Ferry suffers three serious accidents over three consecutive years in the late 1930s. In 1938, a hurricane destroys the passenger launch, and while Tony builds a replacement on the Point, a substitute provided by the town breaks down four times on the day it begins service in 1939. It also rocks frighteningly while loading. And it leaks. Tony abandons it that first afternoon.

But the boat he builds lasts only two days longer. It has the same flat-ended bow as the *City of Chappaquiddick*, so it can load passengers from the ramps the way the ferry loads cars. But there are signs that Tony has rushed the job. The engine is uncovered and it smokes. Apparently the craft carries no life jackets or anchor and possibly goes into service on August 9, 1939, without inspection or a license.

Three midnights later, with his nephew Foster Silva at the helm, there is a burst of flame from the engine, and then another. Six passengers heading back to Chappy in evening dress jump into the harbor, Foster jumping, too. Most swim to what is now Memorial Wharf and cling to the spiles.

Walstein Osborn, a Chappy ferryman from twenty years before, hears the distress, boards a skiff at his father Charlie's boathouse, and rows to the glow in the night, rescuing four of the six swimmers. The other two are hauled up to the pier by ropes.

Joined by three crewman, Hollis Fisher, skipper of the Edgartown Yacht Club launch, steams out to the passenger scow, hooks it while still aflame, and tows it to the Point. Once ashore in Edgartown, Foster Silva starts up the *City of Chappaquiddick* and takes a crew of firemen over to the Point, where they put out the conflagration.

Tony commissions Manuel Swartz Roberts to build a new replacement, which he calls *Sleepy*. Yet with the Depression on the wane and more and more cars crossing every year, the *Sleepy* is the last passenger launch to serve the Chappaquiddick ferry.

VINEYARD GAZETTE

ar; 5c a Copy. Eight Pages.

Seven Leap for Lives From Burning Ferry

Prompt and Heroic Rescue Work Alone Prevents Tragedy in Edgartown Harbor on Saturday Night

A sudden burst of flame forced six passengers and the ferryman to leap for their lives from the Chappaquiddick ferry into Edgartown Harbor soon after midnight Saturday. A rapid dash to the rescue by Walstein Osborn, the coolness of the acting ferryman, Foster Silva, and of the passengers themselves, and the prompt work of Hollis Fish[illegible]

Manuel and Tony begin to build the ferry of oak on the harbor side of Chappy Point in September 1934, with Lawrence Jeffers, Oscar Johanson, and Jesse Jeffers, all of Chappy, helping out as needed. The boat is built upside down to make it easy to plank the bottom. When the time comes to turn it over, Manuel fits the boat with a bridle. Tony asks the foreman of a jetty-building project for help, and the foreman tows a gigantic barge with a seventy-five-foot crane to the Point.

"He grabbed hold of that raft just like a toothpick," says Tony. "I never saw anything like it." The crane raises the ferry high in the air, turns her right side up, lowers her onto a set of blocks, and there she lies on the beach, "pretty as a picture."

BETTENCOURT FAMILY

Tony Bettencourt in 1947, his last full year of service.

Jesse Jeffers, a mechanic, installs an old ninety-horsepower Chrysler Ace automobile engine in the ferry, which measures thirty feet long, twelve feet across, and three feet below the waterline. With a propeller at one end only, and an upright tiller on the starboard side, the new ferry would have to back out of her slip and turn around every time she makes the trip across. Cars would drive on forward but back off the boat.

Manuel, Tony, and the crew plank the deck, build seats and railings along the sides, and on Sunday, May 12, 1935, the foreman returns with his barge to lift the ferry from the beach to the water. Just before he does, Dr. William Andrews, a summer resident of Chappaquiddick, offers to bet Tony $20—about $330 today

"Doc, I wouldn't dare to bet," says Tony. "I don't know if it will work or not myself. This is sort of a little invention of my own."

The *City of Chappaquiddick* steams toward Edgartown early in her career, a 1934 Ford truck on deck.

ROY MEEKINS

and conceivably a year's profit for the ferry during the Depression—that the new boat will never work.

BETTENCOURT FAMILY

Resting on a marine railway during World War II, the *City of Chappaquiddick* shows off the ingenious underwater design of skeg and propeller that enables her to run under her own power.

"Doc, I wouldn't dare to bet," says Tony. "I don't know if it will work or not myself. This is sort of a little invention of my own." The new ferry settles on the harbor, low and sleek, her bow and stern cut sharply inward to help tamp down the chop as she sails back and forth. For a scow she looks almost racy.

Family and friends fill her deck for a shakedown cruise over the harbor. "I got into it, pressed the button on the old Chrysler, and off she went," says Tony. "Oh boy!"

"I got into it, pressed the button on the old Chrysler and off she went," says Tony. "Oh boy!"

He turns circles and steams all across the harbor, answering celebratory whistles with a whistle on the ferry. The skeg keeps her course straight and true. She is launched with an offhand name, *Chappy*. But Joseph Chase Allen, waterfront columnist for the *Vineyard Gazette*, believes that with a ferry like this on the route, the little island that once aspired to become its own town can begin to think even bigger thoughts. That's how the new boat comes to be called the *City of Chappaquiddick*.

But the very existence of such a boat confounds the Commonwealth of Massachusetts.

When Tony appears at the customhouse in Boston to register the ferry as a commercial vessel, officials can't understand what he's talking about. They have never heard of a barge with its own engine, and they instruct him to return with pictures of the ferry doing her job to prove that she actually works.

When the state finally grants the registration a year later—her passengers entrusting themselves, their families, and cars to an unlicensed boat all that time—it must create a whole new classification for the *City of Chappaquiddick*, as well as any craft that might ever follow her innovative design: "motor scow."

With the appearance of the new ferry, what remains of the need for complete self-reliance on Chappaquiddick vanishes altogether. For a price, it is now possible to cross to Edgartown on foot or by car at any hour of the day or night. But under Tony Bettencourt the ferry sails on—for a little while longer—with an old-world air of welcome, improvisation, and adventure.

The Most Spectacular Collision

The witnesses to the disaster could never have forgotten what they saw that midsummer evening. Even today it ranks as the most unlikely and spectacular collision ever to occur in Edgartown Harbor.

At about half-past seven on the evening of Friday, July 23, 1937, a Travel Air 6000 B seaplane carrying one pilot and five passengers on a charter from New Bedford lands inside the entrance to the harbor. It is the end of the first day of the Edgartown Yacht Club regatta, one of the busiest sailing afternoons of the summer. Yet seaplanes land at the gateway to the harbor and moor within it all year-round.

ROY MEEKINS

Taxiing swiftly toward the narrows where the ferry sails back and forth, Alfred R. Leckshied, the pilot, sees the *City of Chappaquiddick* departing the Edgartown slip. He tries to turn to the left, but the wind and current carry the plane to the right.

"It was an awful sight to see that propeller grinding toward us," says Foster Silva, the skipper of the ferry that day. Aboard is Malcolm Keniston at the wheel of a laundry truck and on foot is Charles B. Johnson, a butler for a summer family on Chappy. Foster yells to both men to jump. Malcolm and Foster go over the side just as a pontoon hits the ferry and the right wing strikes the truck, knocking it over onto the railing. Charles, who cannot swim well, is swept into the water by the crash, his face badly cut.

The plane begins to sink nose first and upside down, but as it drifts by Memorial Wharf, two bosuns from a Coast Guard patrol boat at the pier lasso the tail and tie it to a piling. Two civilians and a third bosun jump into the water and with knives and axes begin to hack through the fabric-covered fuselage to reach the passengers in the cabin, which is filling with water. Coast Guardsmen on the boats add lines to the tail, and bystanders and police on the wharf add muscle to the effort to keep the plane afloat.

A damaged Robbins Laundry truck from Falmouth.

ROY MEEKINS

Wrecked seaplane raised as the Vineyard Gazette *heralds the story.*

The pilot and three passengers escape through windows. The two remaining passengers crawl through the hole cut through the tail. Those from the ferry—Foster, Malcolm, and Charles—are picked up from the harbor by boats. The *City of Chappaquiddick*, a seat and railing damaged, resumes service the next day.

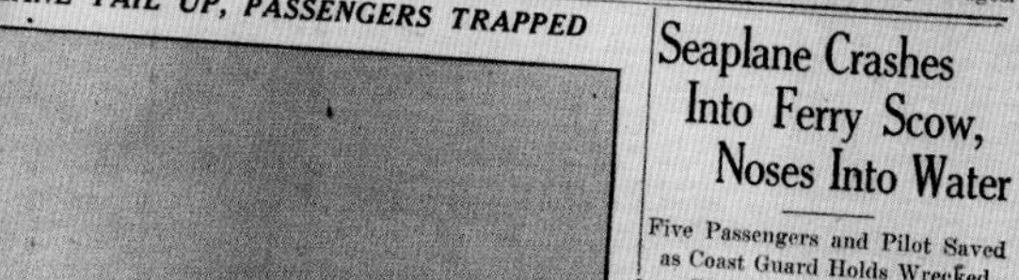

SS., TUESDAY, JULY 27, 1937 $2.50 a Year; 5c a Copy. Eight Pages.

PLANE TAIL UP, PASSENGERS TRAPPED

Photograph by Alfred Wannamaker.

Through a hole in the tail of this wrecked seaplane, Mrs. Johnfritz Achelis and James T. Baldwin were rescued after the crash at Edgartown Friday evening. The picture was taken after the rescue, as the baggage of passengers was taken out of the wreck. The plane was prevented by coastguardsmen from being swept away in the strong tide.

Seaplane Crashes Into Ferry Scow, Noses Into Water

Five Passengers and Pilot Saved as Coast Guard Holds Wrecked Craft Fast to Wharf—None Seriously Injured

Three Dive to Rescue

Men on Ferry Jump, One Is Swept Off by Plane and Badly Hurt—Plane Pilot Says the Rudder Failed

Skimming in over the water of Edgartown harbor, a seaplane headed directly for the Chappaquiddick ferry scow, the pilot unable to make a left turn to clear the ferry and other obstructions, and crashed at about 7:25 Friday evening. Two men dove from the ferry just before the crash occurred, and another was swept into the water by the plane, sustaining severe injuries. Pilot and passengers in the plane escaped serious injury.

The accident occurred just off the dolphin at the northeasterly corner of the steamboat dock. As the wrecked plane, nosing down into the water with pilot and five passengers inside, was being swept by a strong current past the corner of the wharf, United States coastguardsmen seized it and made it fast with a line. This quick action, in a fractional part of a minute after the crash, almost certainly prevented a major tragedy. In another instant or two the wreck would have been swept into deep water and the efforts of rescuers rendered desperate.

Coast Guard Led Rescue

Two civilians and a coastguardsman dove over at the first moment, and coastguardsmen led the work of extricating all the victims of the accident without serious injury. The cour-

s Only 7 Below Record

a brief instant and lost control of his vehicle. The driver was unhurt

VINEYARD GAZETTE

A Ferry Sunk, a Launch Destroyed

The Great New England Hurricane of September 21, 1938, costs the Chappy ferry its passenger launch, which sweeps away from the slip on the Point and smashes into a wooden walkway leading out the old Edgartown Lighthouse, itself damaged beyond repair by the storm.

At the ferry slip on the Point, loose boats, piers, and other wreckage bang into the *City of Chappaquiddick* as the storm surge carries them out of the harbor. To save the ferry, Foster Silva sinks her in the slip before he struggles through the sea to higher ground.

"The next morning was flat calm," says Foster. As he walks back to the ferry, the road is rutted with craters, and on the Point he finds cars upside down and half buried the sand, and boathouses backhanded off their foundations. "I got the *City of Chappaquiddick* up on the beach at high tide and when the tide went out the water'd run out of the ferry," he says. "What didn't, I pumped out. I took the starter and generator off, brought them home, put them in the oven and cooked them out. A day or two later, I had it going again."

On Saturday nights, Tony puts the bow of the ferry against the face of the Edgartown Yacht Club, strides into the clubhouse, and calls out to the Chappy teenagers: "Come on, children, I'm taking you home."

"I remember coming in the summers in our funny car with my brother's crib on the top, and getting down to the ferry, and Tony would come across," says Ann Hoar Floyd, "and oh, my gosh, the welcome we got. It was like coming home to a grandfather. He loved us to pieces. And his favorite thing to say was, 'Hello, children!' It didn't matter whether you were eight months, or eight years, or eighty."

Tony lets youngsters jump from the ferry and swim ashore as she approaches the Point. When there are no cars or passengers waiting—still fairly often, even in summer—he bears off in mid-channel and pulls out hand lines and bait so kids can fish for cunners and scup. As midnight approaches on Saturday nights, he puts the bow of the ferry against the face of the Edgartown Yacht Club, strides into the clubhouse where the young people dance, and calls out to the Chappy teenagers, "Come on, children, I'm taking you home."

Twice married, Tony raises three sons, a daughter, and a stepdaughter in houses on the Chappy hills and waterfront. But the ferry he introduces to Chappaquiddick winds up demanding more of Tony than he is entirely ready to give.

When in the winter of 1948 he requests the first rate hike of his nineteen-year tenure—from six cents per passenger each way to a dime, and fifty cents per car and driver to seventy-five—the county commissioners hear complaints from year-round islanders that he does not always provide the service his boats are able to offer.

"We can wait up to three hours while Tony goes on a shopping tour or is gunning, eating, or feeding his livestock," complains Mrs. Cesar Lopes. "People who have been ill have waited one hour. We want an energetic, conscientious ferryman, and efficient service. Several men are ready to take over any time Tony so desires." He learns that one of these men is his nephew, Foster B. Silva, who has substituted as a captain for his uncle but now quietly tells the commissioners that if he is given the franchise there will be more service and no rise in rates.

On June 30, 1948, Tony, hurt and angered, notifies the commissioners that he intends to resign. They thank him for his service, appoint his nephew Foster to the job, and ask Tony to sell or lease him the *City of Chappaquiddick*.

No dice, says Tony. He will use her as a party boat, taking people to clambakes and picnics, and scallop with her during the winter. The final day of Tony's Ferry will be Sunday, August 1—no give on that date, he insists—leaving Foster Silva only days to figure out how to start up his service when he has no boat to run it.

It also leaves Edgartown with one of the most enduring and erroneous myths of its 350-year history.

Ferry Schedule, 1929–1948

- Likely the same as his predecessor, James Yates:
- Ferry to meet all arriving and departing mainland steamships between 6:00 a.m. and 7:00 p.m. (Steamboat service discontinued after 1934.)
- Ferryman in attendance between 8:00 a.m. and noon, 1:00 p.m.–4:00 p.m., and 5:00 p.m.–7:00 p.m.
- Tony is known to be on call at night

Fares, 1929–1948

- Passenger: $.06 each way (1929 fare is $.79 in 2012 dollars)
- Car and driver: $.50 each way (1929 fare is $6.62 in 2012 dollars)
- Rates double after scheduled hours to midnight
- Subsidy eliminated after 1929

Population on Chappaquiddick, 1940

- Twenty year-round

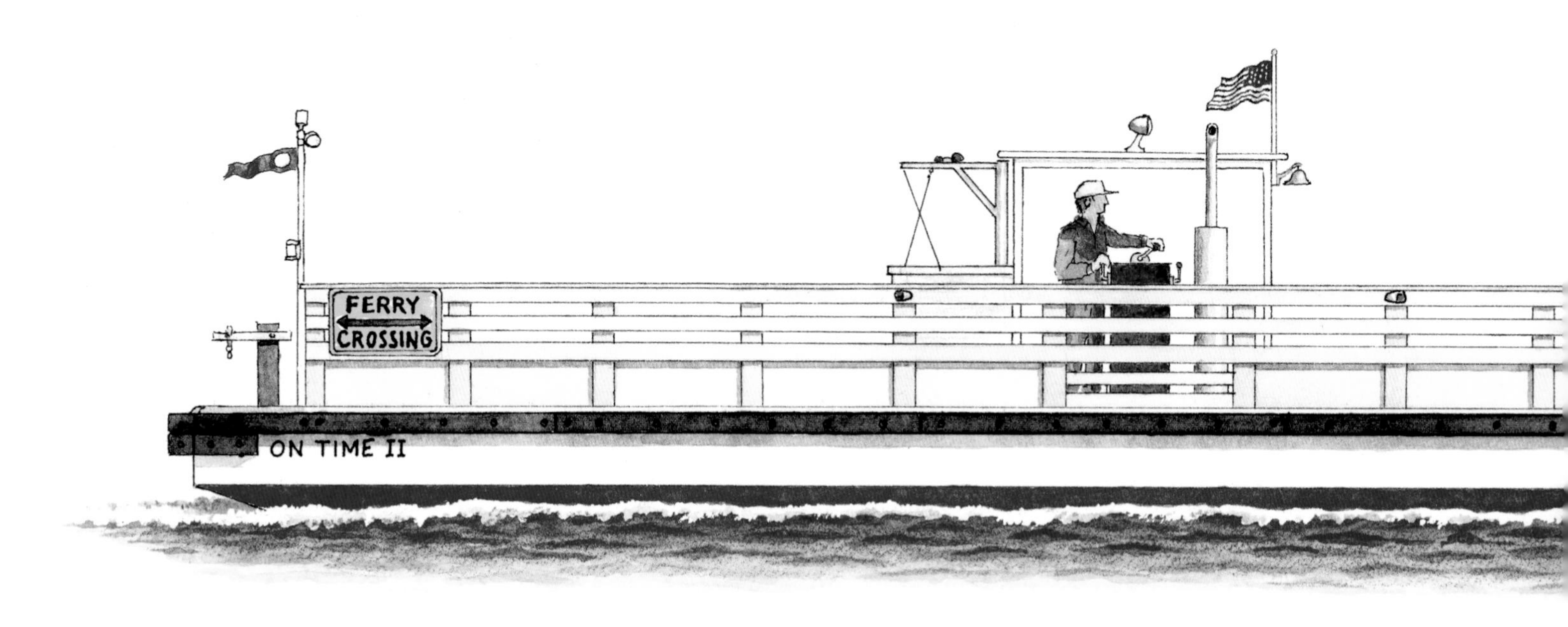

Specifications

ON TIME II:

Length Overall............... **55 feet**
Beam..................... **18 feet**
Draft..................... **4 feet**
Displacement........ **45 tons empty**
Horsepower................. **225**
Propeller...... **32"** diameter, 5 blades

ON TIME III:

Length Overall............. **64 feet**
Beam at Waterline........... **14 feet**
Beam on Deck............. **18 feet**
Draft..................... **4 feet**
Displacement....... **32 tons empty**
Horsepower.................. **225**
Propeller....... **32"** diameter, 5 blades

The **ON TIME II** is heavier than the **ON TIME III** because she floated too high when first launched, and had to have concrete ballast added to achieve the designed waterline. The **III** floated properly at her intended waterline from the start.

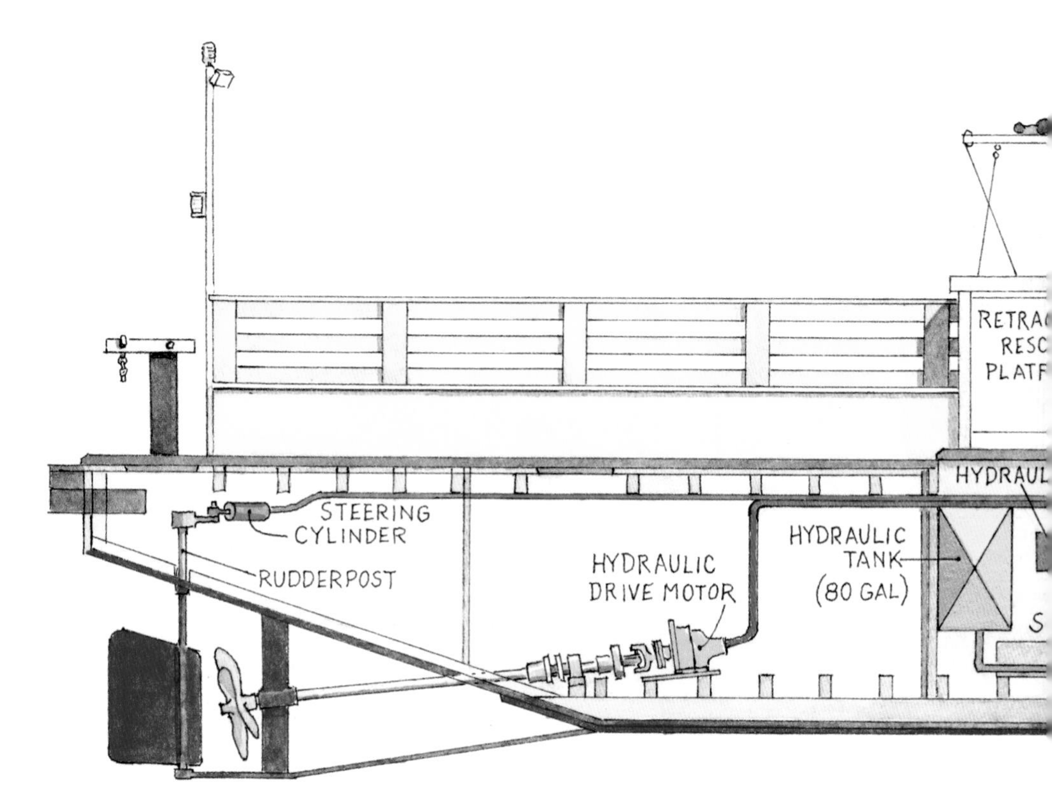

HOW IT WORKS

The ferryboat **ON TIME II** is double-ended: her hull is symmetrical, meaning that both ends are the same. She has a propeller and rudder at each end; this allows her to reverse direction without turning around. The propellers are spun by a **Diesel Hydraulic Propulsion System**:

1) A 225-horsepower John Deere **Diesel Engine** spins a high-pressure, high-volume **Hydraulic Pump**
2) The pump pushes hydraulic oil under great pressure through pipes, hoses, and valves to **Hydraulic Drive Motors** at either end of the ferry
3) The drive motors spin propeller shafts which pass through watertight seals to the underside of the hull
4) At the end of each shaft is a large, 5-bladed propeller which drives the ferry through the water

The captain uses a single lever to control the speed of the ferry by regulating the flow of fuel to the diesel engine, and the direction of the ferry by regulating the **Hydraulic Drive Valve.** This valve sends oil flow to only one of the drive motors at a time. The propellers turn in one direction only: one propeller pushes the ferry out of the slip and across the harbor, then disengages as the ferry approaches the opposite slip. The other propeller then engages to slow the ferry as it eases into the slip.

A smaller hydraulic pump, also spun by the diesel engine, operates the steering system. Hydraulic oil flows from the pump through pipes, hoses, and valves to hydraulic cylinders at each end of the ferry. The captain controls each rudder with an electric steering lever which remotely activates an electronic solenoid. The solenoid opens and closes a valve which directs the flow of hydraulic oil to the steering cylinder; an arm from the cylinder turns the rudderpost, changing the rudder angle to steer the ferry.

The ferryboat **ON TIME III** has an identical propulsion and steering system.

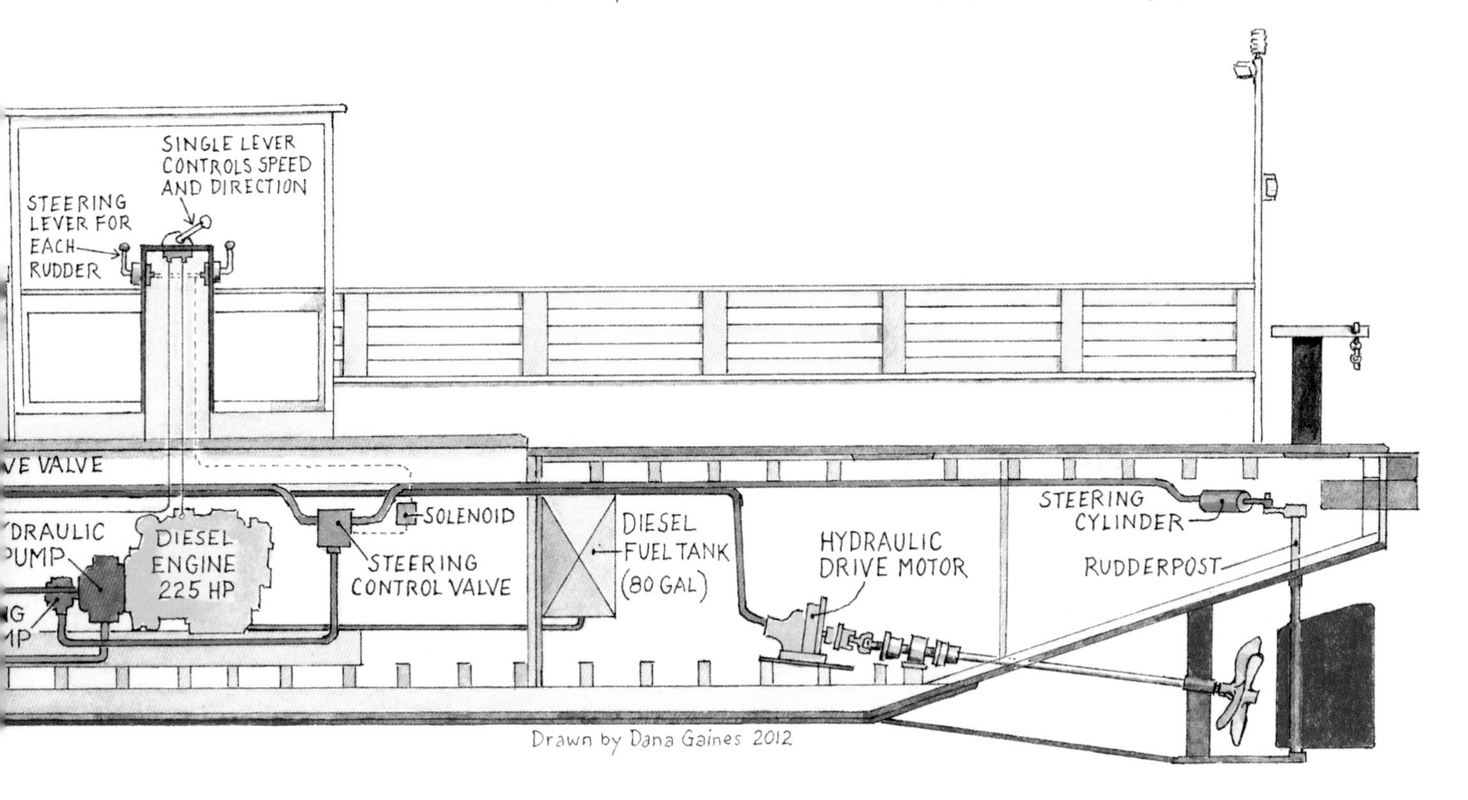

Drawn by Dana Gaines 2012

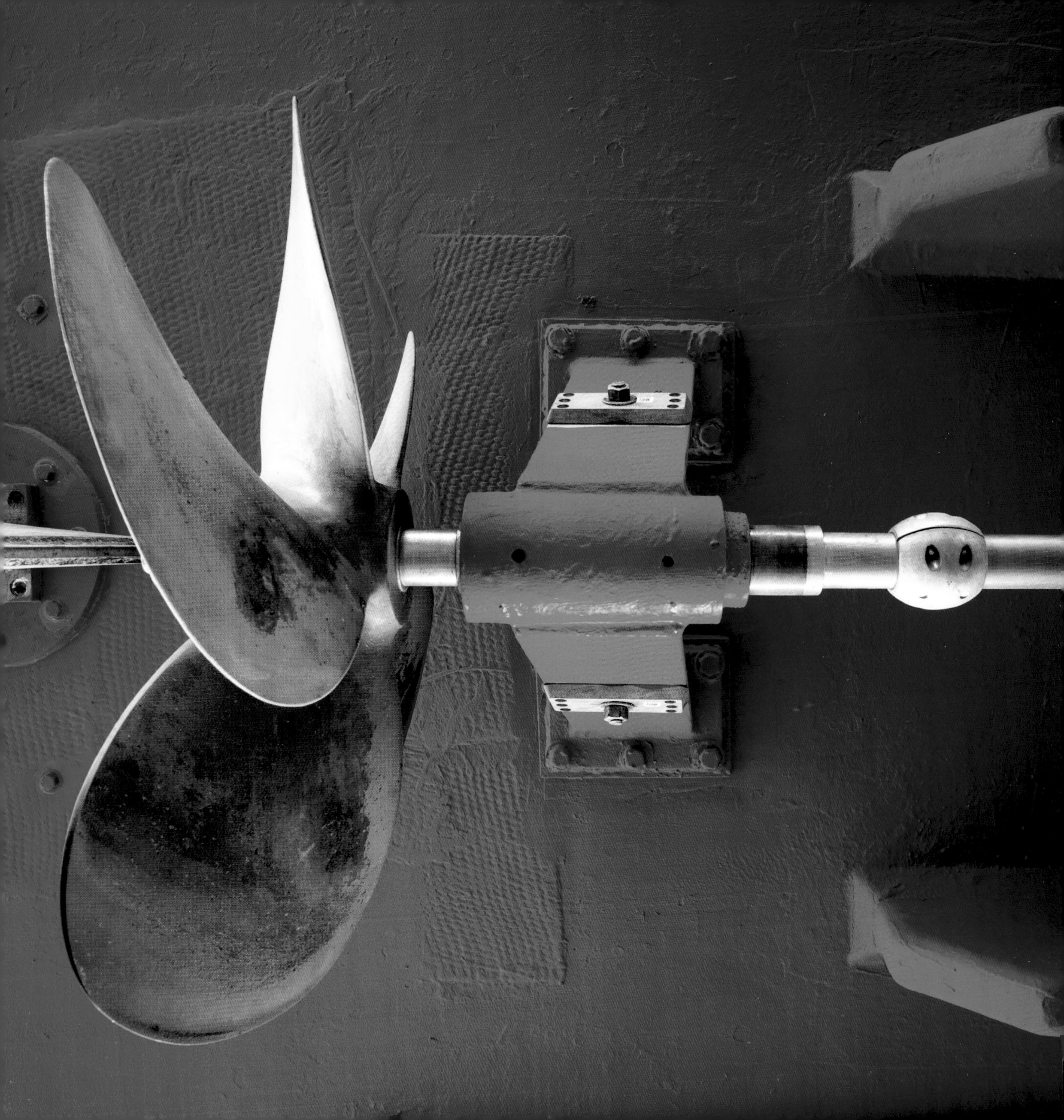

CHAPTER 7

Foster B. Silva

1948–1953

Foster Silva does most everything early and fast.

The son of Manuel S. and Mary Bettencourt Silva, and the nephew of Tony Bettencourt, all of Chappaquiddick, Foster buys his first house on the island at the age of fifteen and begins to fix it up. He marries Odeama (Dodie) Gill of Peabody, Massachusetts, on November 11, 1939. She is sixteen, he twenty-one.

At twenty-four he enlists in the air force, and he is driving a half-track in a Burma jungle when shrapnel from a bomb rips through a slit in the vehicle and blinds him in one eye. With four battle stars on his China-Burma-India ribbon, Foster returns home to Chappaquiddick on the day President Roosevelt dies in 1945.

But Foster never moves faster than he does in the two weeks and six days between Wednesday, July 14, and Monday, August 2, 1948.

VINEYARD GAZETTE

Foster Silva at the helm of the *City of Chappaquiddick*.

Car lines for the ferry, circa 1952.

ROY MEEKINS

Foster Silva never moves faster than he does in the two weeks and six days at the end of July 1948.

SIDNEY N. RIGGS

Edgartown slip, from the end of Memorial Wharf.

The first date is when the county commissioners appoint him Chappaquiddick ferry master. The second is the date he must start. But because Tony Bettencourt believes his nephew has nabbed the service from him, he refuses either to delay his departure or to sell Foster the *City of Chappaquiddick* or passenger launch *Sleepy*. And Foster can't just go to the ferry store and buy replacement boats for a route as narrow, tideswept, and tempestuous as this one often is.

Frantic, Foster turns to Captain Samuel B. Norton of Edgartown, whose skills transcend whole worlds. At sea he dresses in a uniform and serves as captain of the *Manxman*, the largest yawl ever built, among other sailing vessels owned by wealthy families. Ashore, he puts on working clothes, moves houses, and sells lumber and scrap metal as the needs arise. Sam Norton has never built a boat before, but he has spent his life around shipyards, and he tells Foster that he can build a ferry in the time allowed. "Somehow," says Sam's son, Floyd, "he had the ability to do any kind of thing like that."

A Fireman Severely Injured

On the drizzling afternoon of September 22, 1950, a new, twelve-thousand-dollar Edgartown fire truck, headed for a blaze at the farm of Leo Gill on Chappaquiddick, slides backward into the Chappy slip after the chains holding the *On Time* to the ramp snap as the truck tries to climb the damp wooden ramp at low tide. Donald A. Berube, an electrician with a wife and four children, and serving as a volunteer fireman, is severely hurt when his arm is briefly pinned between the fire truck and the ferry.

EDGARTOWN, MARTHA'S VINEYARD, MASS., FRIDAY, SEPTEMBER 29, 1950

ACTION SCENES FOLLOWING EDGARTOWN FIRE TRUCK'S MISHAP

Left: Swamped truck in Chappaquiddick slip as seen from ferry. Right: Side view, looking across slip.

Photographs by Walter Bettencourt of Gazette staff.

Many Gifts to D.C.H.S. Reported by Curator

At Annual Meeting Gookin Reports on Efforts to Counteract "Mistakes and Ineptitud...

about 1900, S. Prescott Fay and Allan Keniston.

A Startling Change Comes to Main Street

Vincent Paper Store Changes Hands; Owned by One Family Half a Century

VINEYARD GAZETTE

"Plan Is to Build New Ferry Scow in 11 Days," reads the headline on the front page of the *Vineyard Gazette* on the morning of Tuesday, July 20, 1948. "As these words are printed, the lumber of which the new craft is to be built is still in the log, but Capt. Samuel B. Norton, who has accepted direction of the project, says, 'On the morning of the 2nd, she'll be ready.'"

Plans for the new ferry are sketched on a paper bag or scrap of paper with the guidance of Manuel Swartz Roberts, who is nearing retirement—and for whom this boat will be the seventh and last in the fleet of Chappy ferries and bathing beach launches that he has built or refit since 1927. The new ferry is to be forty feet long, fourteen feet across the beam, and measure eleven tons.

"Plan Is to Build New Ferry Scow in 11 Days," reads the front-page headline of the Vineyard Gazette.

She will be boxier than the *City of Chappaquiddick*, her deck considerably higher off the water to help keep it dry as she drives through the chop. Though the idea is eventually to install a propeller and rudder at both ends so that the ferry can one day shuttle back and forth without turning around, there is no time to add a second prop and rudder now. For the present at least, she will back out of her slip, pivot, and cross as the *City of Chappaquiddick* does.

At eleven o'clock on the first morning, Sam Norton tells his crew, "This won't be eight-hour days."

On Wednesday, July 21, Sam and Floyd pick up the lumber in Portsmouth, Rhode Island, and an eight-cylinder Chrysler engine in Fairhaven, Massachusetts. Racing for home that evening, they pull over to call the Woods Hole office of the Massachusetts Steamship Lines, which holds the last boat of the night for them.

At eleven o'clock the next morning, Sam stands before his son and seven other men on the south side of the dirt parking lot at Memorial Wharf. With everything they need to build the new ferry stacked around them, Sam tells his crew, "This won't be eight-hour days."

It turns into the harborfront equivalent of a barn-raising. Villagers and summer residents visit the construction site by the score, bringing coffee and donuts in the morning and sandwiches in the afternoon and evening. "They were excited to see all the activity, and they wanted to be part of it," says Floyd. "And they would help. They'd come, and they'd saw the planks, and they'd carry them over." Built upside down as the *City of Chappaquiddick* was over on Chappaquiddick Point thirteen years

Tony and the *City of Chappaquiddick* after Retirement

On the rainy afternoon of Sunday, August 1, 1948, Tony Bettencourt is aboard the *City of Chappaquiddick* in the Edgartown slip. He sees a huge crowd on Chappy Point and heads over to pick them up, believing they have come to watch the launching of the ferry that is to replace his the following morning.

In fact they have come to thank Tony for the service he has offered them for the past nineteen years. In the downpour he takes them on a tour of the harbor, whistle blaring as it did that morning thirteen years before, when he sailed his revolutionary new ferry and some of these very same admirers across the harbor on her shakedown cruise.

As Foster Silva and the new *On Time* take over, Tony uses the former ferry as a party boat.

"Anything he had to do with it to continue to make some money," says his son, Skip Bettencourt. "He used to go scalloping with it, towing drags. We have movies of that—carrying bags of scallops off the ferry. It had a thousand different lives. And people loved that ferry." The *City of Chappaquiddick* keeps working another twenty-eight years.

BETTENCOURT FAMILY

A historic ferry in her final year of service.

ALL PHOTOS: CLARA F. DINSMORE / FLOYD NORTON

The new *On Time* just before her launch at Memorial Wharf, 1948.

before, the new ferry is framed, planked, caulked, and painted in six days. To turn it over, Sam secures it by chains, blocks, and heavy rope to the derrick of his six-wheeled Autocar truck and hauls. But with seven tons of wood and fastenings in the hull already, it is the wheels on the far side of the truck, rather than the scow, which lift.

Floyd anchors the derrick by guy wires to a deadman in the parking lot, and this time the hull rises, rotates, and lands softly on a cushion of air produced by the flat of her bottom as she falls. Francis T. Meyer, a former commodore of the Edgartown Yacht Club, organizes a ceremony for the event, and a green tree is attached to the hull, an ancient symbol of community ownership.

Hull of new ferry is turned over.
Inset: Captain Samuel B. Norton.

On the rainy afternoon of Sunday, August 1, the scow begins to move from the parking lot where she is built. She rests on rollers, and the Autocar pulls and turns her slowly onto Dock Street. With the launching scheduled for high water that evening, men install the engine, machinery, and wiring even as she inches along the road.

She is backed to the water's edge just south of Memorial Wharf, her stern hanging a few feet over the harbor. But it takes more time than expected to install the propeller and rudder. Loyal to his Chappy friends to the last, Tony Bettencourt cheerfully agrees to delay his retirement by twenty-four hours, and the launching occurs the following night.

Excursions of the Open Door Club

In the summer of 1939 a group of African American housekeepers, cooks, and gardeners forms a society called the Open Door Club in Edgartown. Members meet on Thursday and Sunday afternoons, which are known as Maid's Day Off, so that they can enjoy part of a Vineyard summer to themselves. At its most active in the early 1950s, the club counts sixty-five members.

Participants establish a choral group, host lecturers, hold fund-raisers for Vineyard causes, and offer an August afternoon tea for employers and their friends. The club also schedules outings, and among the most popular are excursions aboard the *City of Chappaquiddick* with Tony Bettencourt to South Beach, Bend in the Road beach, and Cape Pogue.

"They had a blast," says Clarence A. (Trip) Barnes III, who is a summer kid on Chappy in those days. "They would fish for scup to make it exciting, and they would be drinking and eating and having picnics" on the old motor scow. This goes on through the late 1950s, when the *City of Chappaquiddick* returns to service as a backup ferry. In 1972, with the retirement of the last of its founders, Mrs. Edna Smith, the Open Door Club disbands.

VINEYARD GAZETTE

Foster Silva is aboard when Mrs. Ruth Letourneau of Chappaquiddick cracks a bottle of Champagne against her bow on Monday evening, August 2. Lit by headlights and flashbulbs, the new ferry slides into the harbor. With a quick Coast Guard inspection, the boat goes into service the following morning.

She carries two cars easily, though her flat bow shovels the water before her and heaves a fair amount of it onto her deck after all. She has an upright tiller like the *City of Chappaquiddick*, but it is much heavier, Foster pushing and pulling with his whole body to turn her left or right. She never gets the second propeller or rudder that would enable her to sail back and forth without having to turn around.

CHANTAL HODGES

Postcard of the *On Time* at the start of her career, circa 1948.

Enlargement of the ferry increases the demand for its service beyond the point Foster Silva wants to offer it.

Foster serves a single five-year term as ferryman. Like his uncle before him, he finds enlargement of the ferry increases the demand for its service beyond the point he wants to offer it. In 1953 he sells the operation and moves with Dodie to Costa Mesa, California, where, ironically, he takes a job skippering a three-car ferry between Balboa Island and Balboa Peninsula, a far busier operation—though often sailed in better weather.

When he returns to Chappaquiddick in 1956 Foster opens a snack bar and an antique shop in Edgartown, serves on the Chappaquiddick fire company, builds and caretakes summer houses, and runs the island landfill.

He is also appointed the first superintendent of the Cape Pogue and Wasque preserves of the Trustees of Reservations, and when visitors marvel at his knowledge of the plants and wildlife to which he introduces them on the shores of Chappaquiddick, he asks them in return, "Don't you know I'm a graduate of Katama University?"

DAVID AND PAT KNOLL

The *On Time* sails across a wide-open harbor entrance in the middle 1950s.

The greatest legacy of the hurried design and speedy construction of the new ferry is a single fact that a resort population, always on the move, begins to forget even before Foster quits. The legend that replaces it is easier to tell—that the new ferry gets its name because it has no schedule and thus is never late. But a few townspeople today, and the ghosts of hundreds who see her launched on the night of August 2, 1948, know the truth, the whole truth, and indeed the only truth:

Because Captain Samuel B. Norton and his crew all but finish construction in the eleven days allowed them, the boxy new ferry is christened *On Time.*

Ferry Schedule, 1948–1953

- Off-season: 7:30 a.m.–6:00 p.m.
- Summer: 7:30 a.m.–midnight
- On call after scheduled hours

Fares, 1953

- Passenger: $.10 each way ($.85 in 2012 dollars)
- Car and driver: $.50 each way ($4.24 in 2012 dollars)
- Rates double after scheduled hours

Population on Chappaquiddick, 1948

- Twelve estimated, year-round

Boats Built or Rebuilt by Manuel Swartz Roberts for the Chappy Ferry and Bathing Beach Launches, 1927–1948

SALLY SANIUTA

- Refits and rebuilds bathing beach launch *Charlesbank*, 1924–1953
- Builds first barge to carry a car, 1927
- Builds unnamed passenger launch, 1929
- Builds Chappy ferry *City of Chappaquiddick*, 1935
- Builds bathing beach launch *Ann*, mid-1930s
- Builds Chappy ferry launch *Sleepy*, 1940–1941
- Helps to design and build Chappy ferry *On Time*, 1948

CHAPTER 8

George T. Silva
1953–1962

"He was a tough son of a bitch to work for," says Robert J. Carroll, who as a young man helps George T. Silva build piers, bulkheads, and stone jetties in Edgartown and other harbors around the Vineyard. "You got tongue-lashed all the time."

Because there are so many George Silvas, living and dead, in Edgartown and all across the Island, he is known as George T. his whole life long. Born June 12, 1901, he is one of the seven sons and six daughters of Antone T. and Mary Tavas Silva, who emigrate from San Miguel in the Azores and settle in Christiantown at the western end of the Island.

"A bull of a guy," remembers Floyd Norton—the sort of man who insists that he and his crew load boulders onto his scow by hand so that he can get the feel of the stone before he fits it into a breakwater. If a boulder falls into deep water or even just lands wrong on a jetty, he tears into the culprit but then feels bad about it at the end of the day and pays everybody off—throwing in a beer, too, with the hope that they will all return to work the next morning. It is a rare day when they do not.

George T. Silva, winter of 1976.

The *On Time*, circa 1960, with the bathing beach launch *Charlesbank*, right.

BETTENCOURT FAMILY

Because there are so many George Silvas, living and dead, in Edgartown and all across the Island, he is known as George T. his whole life long.

It is the first time on record that a Chappy ferryboat changes hands from one owner to the next.

As harbormaster, George T. is already the most influential man on the waters of Edgartown when he buys the *On Time* from Foster Silva—no relation—for an unknown sum and takes over the license on December 29, 1953. It is the first time on record that a Chappy ferryboat changes hands from one owner to the next.

But George T. feels no particular call to own the ferry and never skippers it; indeed, he gives up swordfishing as a young man because he gets seasick. But he has a daughter, Priscilla; a small granddaughter, Barbara; and a son-in-law, George Magnuson Jr., who wants to build houses. George T. thinks young George, who serves in the merchant marine during World War II, can run the ferry until he establishes himself as a contractor in Edgartown.

It is a period of subtle transitions all across the Vineyard. During the war, officers and enlisted men train at the Martha's Vineyard Naval Air Auxiliary Facility—now the airport—or practice landings on Island beaches ahead of D-Day, and they fall in love with the Vineyard. Now, after the war, many return with their families to spend all or part of the summer. Fishermen bring their families to vacation on Chappy, too,

Foundering under the Weight of a Lumber Truck

VINEYARD GAZETTE

On June 18, 1958, a truck overloaded with lumber from Falmouth slides to one side of the *On Time* in her Edgartown slip, spilling her cargo into the harbor and causing the ferry to take on water through a vent. Workmen from Norton and Easterbrooks Boatyard (now Edgartown Marine) cut a hole in the deck to pump her out. The old *City of Chappaquiddick*, reacquired by George T. Silva as a backup ferry, offers assistance. After this accident, drivers must certify the weights of their trucks before they board the ferry.

VINEYARD GAZETTE

Winds and currents shift broken fields of ice at the entrance to Edgartown Harbor. The *On Time II* sails around the hazards on her way to the Point.

after what is originally called the Martha's Vineyard Striped Bass Derby introduces them to the fishing grounds off East Beach and Wasque Point beginning in 1946.

Edgartown and Chappaquiddick do not fear overbuilding or even overcrowding—yet. There remains more than enough room for everyone, even in summer, and something of a rivalry remains among Island towns to see where a beautiful new seasonal home will be built next.

What worries summer residents and a few Islanders is what they see happening on the nearby mainland. All along the once quiet, winding roads of Cape Cod, motels and motor homes suddenly appear, along with clam bars and hotdog stands—evidence to some Vineyarders that the Cape is devolving into just another modern "cheap resort."

They look across the Island, see a landscape almost completely unprotected by regulations of any kind, and begin to fear that the same sort of uncontrolled, rapid, and permanent change may swiftly remake the Vineyard. There are concerns on Chappy, too. Fearing commercial development of almost any kind, and for the third time since the attempt to separate from Edgartown twenty-five years before, summer residents in 1951 form an island association to help "preserve Chappaquiddick in the form which it was when it attracted all of us to it."

A Ferryman at the Oars Again

Working once more as a captain on the Chappy ferry, Tony Bettencourt and his son, Skip, ferry Mrs. William West to Chappy in the late 1950s, probably while the *On Time* undergoes spring maintenance. In 1957 George T. Silva buys the *City of Chappaquiddick* from Tony to run as a backup ferry when the *On Time* breaks down or is laid up for her annual overhaul.

MARTHA'S VINEYARD MUSEUM

Though George T. hires additional captains—Tony Bettencourt begins to fill in again after his nephew Foster sells the ferry—for George Magnuson the job is beyond boring. Often in winter, nobody shows up all day until he goes home for supper, when someone inevitably calls for a trip across. In summer the pace is relentless, the passengers not always friendly by day and not always sober by night. "All this stuff was adding up, adding up, till I couldn't wait to get away from the damn thing," he says.

For most of the George T. ownership, though, year-round Chappaquiddickers put up with off-season inconveniences that look back almost to the rowboat era. In winter there is no service between 6 p.m. and 7:30 a.m., except by "special arrangement." And until George T. buys and refits the old *City of Chappaquiddick* as a reserve ferry in 1957, there is no boat whatsoever to transport cars for up to ten days in the spring while the *On Time* is hauled out of the water for yearly maintenance.

JERRY GRANT

In the George T. era, horses can still enjoy the open deck as people do.

George Magnuson leaves the ferry and with a partner, Sherman Burnham, soon starts the contracting business of Burnham and Magnuson in Edgartown. George T. sells the ferry in the winter of 1962 and retires as harbormaster in 1968 after serving in the post for twenty-three years. He also retires from the business of building piers and jetties. But he takes up one last great project before his death on June 30, 1986: closing an opening through an ocean-facing beach with his own two hands.

In 1969 South Beach finally seals itself after being open to the Atlantic for most of the previous half-century. But on the night of February 2, 1976, a gale blasts it open once again, separating Chappaquiddick from the rest of the Vineyard and making it an island once more. George T., who is in Florida, flies home the next day. Long experience as harbormaster, pier builder, and ferry owner tells him that the vigorous, swirling currents through Edgartown harbor will overwhelm recreational sailors when summer comes and—contrary to the old belief—damage the shellfish beds in Katama Bay.

For weeks, and often on his own at the age of seventy-five, George T. fills and drags sandbags weighing up to 135 pounds each across the beach to try to close off the opening between bay and ocean. It measures more than a hundred yards across. He hires tractors and front-end loaders to bulldoze it shut. But nature refuses to yield, the opening refuses to close, and in June he gives up.

A few weeks later he submits a bill for $4,032.70 to the county, which owns the beach, for expenses incurred. The commissioners mull over an invoice for a project they didn't order or even consider—and which, in the end, does not work. Then they decide to pay it.

Considering his lifetime of service to the town, they cannot come up with a reason to turn down a bill submitted by George T. Silva.

Ferry Schedule, 1953–1962

- Off-season: 7:30 a.m.–6:00 p.m.
- Summer: 7:30 a.m.–midnight
- On call after scheduled hours

Fares, 1953–1962

- Passenger: $.10 each way (1962 fare is $.75 in 2012 dollars)
- Car and driver: $.50 each way (1962 fare is $3.75 in 2012 dollars)
- Rates double after scheduled hours

Population on Chappaquiddick, 1960

- Twenty-five estimated, year-round

ON TIME II
JIM-BUOY
The Rough Neck

CHAPTER 9

Laurence A. Mercier

1962–1966

LARRY MERCIER

Above: Laurence A. Mercier in 1969.

Below: The first discounted tickets, two cents off.

In these final few years of quiet—before tragedy and a whirlwind of consequences sweep across Chappaquiddick—things are still manageable enough that the ferry can pass without concern to a twenty-one-year-old Edgartown man who spends fully a quarter of his ownership serving as a private in the army on the mainland. He is the youngest Chappy ferry owner on record, his time with the ferry the briefest we know of.

Laurence A. Mercier is the son of Herbert R. and Mary Veronica (Vera) Mercier, grocers who move from Somerville, Massachusetts, in 1939 to run the First National store at the corner of Main and Summer streets in Edgartown. Larry is born August 10 the following year.

After school, he loves to ride back and forth with Richard Bettencourt, oldest son of Tony, who skippers the *On Time* for Foster Silva and George T. Silva and lets Larry raise and lower the ramps and hook up the chains that secure the ferry in the slips. When Larry is older he scallops from a boat and works with George T. building piers and jetties.

He is palling around with friends attending college in Boston late in the winter of 1962, but he wants to own an Island business. He gets a call from Bob Carroll, co-owner of Carroll and Vincent Real Estate, saying that George T. wants to sell the Chappy ferry. Larry comes home from Boston one weekend and learns that George T. wants $20,000 for it—about $150,000 today. "Twenty thousand dollars!" gasps Larry. He wavers.

"But Bob's quite a talker," he says. "He can talk a dog off a meat wagon. So I guess he probably convinced me." Larry decides to buy it before Monday rolls around. His father lends him the down payment, and Larry agrees to pay $5,000 per year in principal and

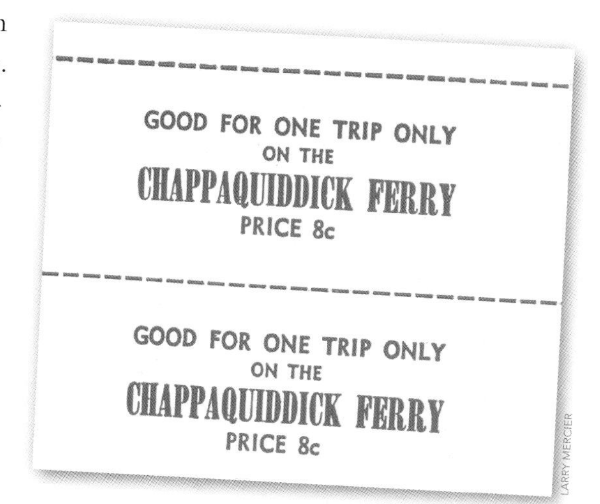

LARRY MERCIER

LARRY MERCIER

The *City of Chappaquiddick*, late in her career as a reserve ferry, circa 1965.

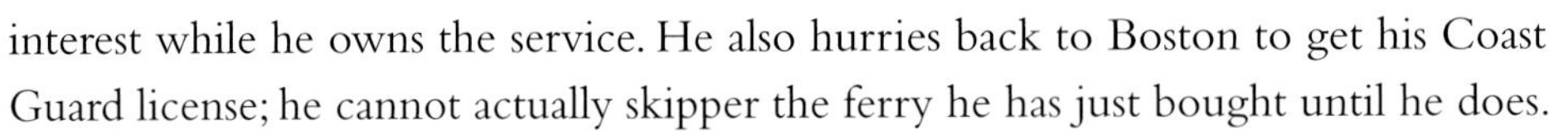

interest while he owns the service. He also hurries back to Boston to get his Coast Guard license; he cannot actually skipper the ferry he has just bought until he does.

Drafted that fall, he serves much of the time as quartermaster aboard an experimental landing ship-tank carrying arms between Charleston, South Carolina, and Newport News, Virginia. It is the first time the ferry is owned from afar, his brother, Herbert Jr., running the business and a captain, John A. Willoughby, looking after the *On Time* and *City of Chappaquiddick*. His father and mother set up their own grocery in town, and Larry returns from the service to take over Mercier's Market on the death of his father in 1964.

Larry comes to realize that selling groceries is his first love, and when he marries Doris McNeil, an X-ray technician, in January 1966, he begins to look for a buyer for the ferry. After he sells it, Larry and Doris have four children while Larry runs markets in both Vineyard Haven and Edgartown. Over time he also serves as selectman, assessor, refuse district committeeman, tree warden, and for twenty-one years, highway superintendent.

At the Helm: John A. Willoughby

As a boy in Edgartown in the 1920s, he rows blocks of ice and bottles of milk from the family farm at Green Hollow across the harbor to customers on Chappy. He earns a license to skipper any vessel of any size on any ocean at the amazingly young age of twenty-eight.

Larry Mercier hires him to captain the Chappy ferry in 1963, and he becomes legendary for the accuracy of his weather forecasts and the singsong lilt of his Edgartown-accented warning to passengers boarding or disembarking the *On Time*: "Watch out for the caahs, folks!"

Captain John A. Willoughby is a quiet man—short, stocky, straight-backed, precise, seldom seen without his Greek fishing cap. "He could come across as harsh at times, and much of his thinking had an Old Testament fire and fury to it," writes Pia Webster after his death in 1999. But he reassures new captains when they botch their first attempts to put the *On Time* in a slip. "If you can walk away from it," he says, "it was a good landing."

A widower and the father of three when he retires from the ferry in the spring of 1977, John is honored with a surprise party at the old Daggett House, just up the street from the Edgartown slip. Friends see no sense in giving a gold watch to a man of the sea or a self-taught meteorologist of such reliable skill. They give him a recording barometer instead.

ERIC SUNDIN

Edgartown is now more responsible for the ferry than at any time in history.

The ferry crosses two significant meridians during the short stewardship of Larry Mercier.

He removes the old gasoline engine from the *On Time* and installs a 125-horsepower Ford Lehman diesel, the first in a Chappy ferry. And through an act signed by the governor in May 1962, oversight of the ferry passes from the county to the one town in which the whole operation runs: Edgartown. The village is now more responsible for the ferry than at any time in history. It owns the slips, ramps, and ferryhouses; regulates the rates; and appoints the ferry master, who continues to own and maintain the ferries himself.

In this hurtling, booming interstate era, Islanders now worry less about the cheapening effects of resorthood and more about the smothering effects of it. As summertime crowds swell and the pace of change quickens, the Vineyard begins

Fate of the Bathing Beach Launches

The bathing beach launches, which siphon away so much business from Charlie Osborn and Jimmy Yates in the first quarter of the twentieth century, sail on together through 1944, when a hurricane brings down a storage shed on the *Irene*, crushing her while she is laid up on Chappaquiddick. A former navy launch, the *Charlesbank* is condemned and broken up by the Martha's Vineyard Shipyard in 1963, the year the bathing beach becomes the privately run Chappaquiddick Beach Club. The fate of the smallest launch, named *Ann*, is unknown.

PHOTO: RUTH WELCH/COURTESY HATSY POTTER

Bathing beach launch Irene, *summer of 1941.*

to feel the same loss of insularity during the Mercier ownership that Chappy feels after the first car hoots its way over the dirt roads of the island back in the summer of 1912.

On Memorial Day weekend 1965, the number of automobile reservations to the Vineyard is up 33 percent over the previous year. Hydrofoil passenger service from Woods Hole is planned for 1966, jet service from New York for 1968. Larry Mercier carries the first trailer truck over to Chappaquiddick—significantly, it is a moving van—and soon the *On Time* is ferrying loads the *City of Chappaquiddick* never manages in its lifetime, including cement trucks that pour foundations for houses rising suddenly and assertively on the beaches, bluffs, and heights of Chappy.

Larry Mercier carries the first trailer truck over to Chappaquiddick—and soon the On Time *is ferrying loads the* City of Chappaquiddick *never manages in its lifetime.*

Ferries to the Fun Zone

At first glance they look like California clones of the Chappaquiddick ferry, crossing an eight-hundred-foot route between Balboa, a manmade island crowded with cottages in the heart of Newport Harbor, and a peninsula that wraps around the harbor and island, protecting both from the Pacific Ocean.

Joseph A. Beek—originally from Maine, an early developer of Balboa Island, and for many years secretary of the state senate—officially founds the modern Balboa ferry with an eighteen-foot outboard launch named *Ark* in 1919.

Today three nearly identical ferries—the *Admiral* of 1953, *Captain* of 1955, and *Commodore* of 1957—sail from the island to the peninsula, landing next door to a small amusement park called the Balboa Fun Zone.

To veterans of the Chappy service, it is strange to see the Balboa boats at work. They look like the Chappy ferries, but sail on busier water and between busier places. And often there are three boats on the job rather than two—one loading and unloading in either slip while the third cruises slowly, easily across a placid bay, waiting for her chance to land.

As a business, the Chappaquiddick ferry is more than twice as old, but because Jerry Grant models the *On Time III* on the hull form of the Balboa boats, they are, in a sense, older sisters doing the same tough job—but in a mellow Southern California spirit.

TOM DUNLOP

PAINTING BY MEG MERCIER

Across most of the Island and all of Edgartown, there is no zoning of land whatsoever; the only regulation standing between a developer and nearly all of the wide-open, unbroken landscape is the issuance of a building permit. Chappaquiddickers look over the confines of their separated island—only five miles by three at the farthest points—and more than ever worry that a fight to protect the shoreline and old rural prospects could be lost before it even begins.

In 1965 more than 90 percent of the landowners on Chappy, both year-round and seasonal, endorse a proposal to zone the entire island as a residential district, with exceptions made for small home enterprises in the ancient Chappy tradition. Edgartown approves a zoning by-law for Chappaquiddick in 1966 and follows suit with zoning regulations of its own on March 12, 1969. Some citizens leave the town meeting that night thinking that this vote may turn out to be the most significant thing that happens in Edgartown all year.

It is not.

Ferry Schedule, 1962–1966

- Off-season: 7:30 a.m.–6:00 p.m.
- Summer: 7:30 a.m.–midnight
- On call after scheduled hours

Fares, 1962–1966

- Passenger: $.10 each way (1966 fare is $.70 in 2012 dollars)
- Car and driver: $.50 each way ($3.49 in 2012 dollars)
- In summer, rates double from 7:30 p.m. to midnight
- Off-season, rates double after scheduled hours

Population on Chappaquiddick, 1963

- Twenty-five estimated, year-round

ON TIME II

CHAPTER 10

Jared N. Grant
1966–1988

When Jerry Grant buys the Chappy ferry in the early spring of 1966, it would be hard to find a person living much beyond New England who has ever seen or heard of it. But before his ownership is half over, it would be harder still to find a person on Earth who hasn't.

Jared N. Grant is born June 16, 1940, the son of Helen Augusta Grant and adopted son of Kenneth W. Grant, who returns from the war to join the partnership of his brothers Ralph and Mansfield, founders of a general contracting company in Edgartown.

Like Larry Mercier, a high school classmate, Jerry is a young man who wants to own a business, and he is running machinery for Grant Brothers when Larry sells him the ferry for $55,000—about $385,000 today—in the first week of April 1966. In the four years Larry owns it, the value of the business nearly triples.

DEBBIE GRANT

Jerry Grant

JERRY GRANT

Jerry Grant during the construction of the *On Time III* in the spring of 1975.

In the four years Larry Mercier owns the ferry, the value of the business nearly triples.

A Summer Night Like No Other

The night of July 18, 1969, is muggy and still. As is often the case when he shuts down the ferry after a busy summer night, Jerry Grant is wound up. He knows it will do him no good to go home and try to sleep. So as is his custom at midnights like this, he walks over to Memorial Wharf with a few ropes and begins to splice, hoping to catch the hint of a cool breeze off the harbor and let the day go.

Six hours before, just as Jerry's shift starts, Senator Edward Kennedy walks aboard the *On Time*, headed for a party with friends at a rented cottage on Chappaquiddick. The departing skipper, the late Dick Hewitt, points him out. "So I looked over—yes, that's Kennedy," recalls Jerry. "I didn't think anything about it."

Later, in a statement televised to his constituents, the senator says that after the car accident he eventually asks a cousin and a friend to drive him to Chappaquiddick Point. Rather than summon the ferry or call the police from the pay phone in the ferryhouse, he says, "I suddenly jumped into the water and impulsively swam across, nearly drowning once again in the effort." He finds his way to his room at the Shiretown Inn, where he collapses in bed about 2 a.m.

Jerry is splicing lines at the end of the wharf until one o'clock in the morning, perhaps later. In that time, over on the Point, nothing happens. "I'd have seen cars," he says. "There were no cars down there." He finally goes home on the quietest of summer nights. For the rest of the time he owns the ferry, he never knows another night quite like it.

EDITH BLAKE/COURTESY MV MUSEUM

Senator and Mrs. Kennedy on the steps of the county courthouse.

Jerry is not yet twenty-six or a man of the water when he takes over the ferry—"I didn't even know what the red buoy meant out there," he says of the channel marker off the harbor light. Also like Larry he must earn a license from the Coast Guard before he can skipper the ferries he has just bought.

"I didn't even know what the red buoy meant out there," says Jerry Grant as he takes over the Chappy ferry.

But he sees right away that he needs a new boat. The reserve ferry *City of Chappaquiddick* is thirty-one years old and wearing out. And the *On Time* often struggles to keep up with the cars and crowds she now carries in the summer.

"We were getting some long lines, even before the Kennedy thing," says Jerry. "Especially on Chappaquiddick. Everybody would come back at 4:30—workmen, everybody else. And with just a two-car ferry, and you had to turn it around—everything took time."

He hires John W. Gilbert, a marine architect from Boston specializing in fishing boats and other commercial vessels, to design a three-car ferry, fifty-five feet long. She will be built of marine plywood and fiberglass laid over fir framing. With two helms and a propeller and rudder at both ends, she will be the first Chappy ferry to sail across the channel without turning around, her cars driving forward, on and off.

Tony Bettencourt sees that the ferry is too light to float where she should. He looks up at Jerry: "Ain't gonna work, Cap," he declares.

In July 1969 Jerry is building the boat at his home in Katama. He works on the deck one afternoon when Tony Bettencourt visits. The man who revolutionized the Chappy ferry thirty-five years before surveys the new hull. Rather than having a flat bottom with a skeg to keep her on course, like the *City of Chappaquiddick*, the bottom of the new ferry is shaped in a deep V, which might conceivably be even more effective.

But it will also make the hull quite buoyant, and what Tony sees is that there is not enough weight in the ferry to make her float in the water where she should. He looks up at Jerry.

"Ain't gonna work, Cap," he declares.

Jerry has been laboring over the new ferry for two years. He has sunk forty-five thousand dollars into it. He is married and the father of four young children. And he is mortified.

"What do you mean, it ain't gonna work?" he calls down. "It's *gotta* work!"

A Crowning Achievement

Shortly after one o'clock Monday morning, November 2, 1981, Daryl Knight of Chappaquiddick realizes her second child is rapidly on the way.

Her husband, Dick Knight, calls Jack Carbon, the overnight captain, at home. Jack races for the *On Time III*, hurries across the channel, and meets the Knights in their Dodge Omni on the Point. Dick is driving, with Daryl in the front seat.

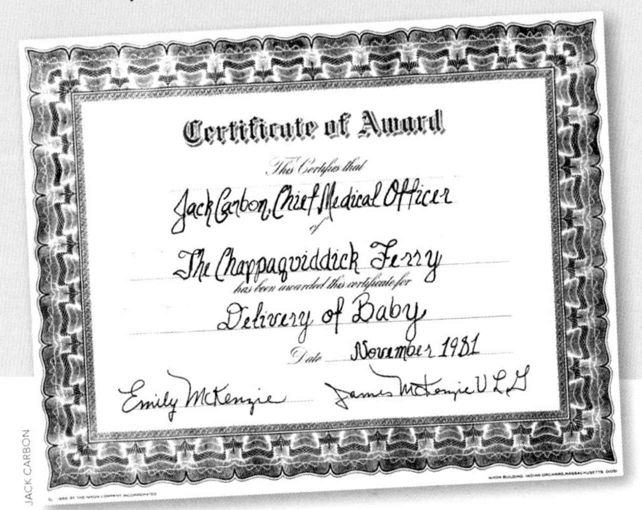

Certificate of Award

This Certifies that

Jack Carbon, Chief Medical Officer

of

The Chappaquiddick Ferry

has been awarded this certificate for

Delivery of Baby

Date November 1981

Emily McKenzie James McKenzie V L G

JACK CARBON

When the ferry pulls into the Edgartown slip, Dick tells Jack to call an ambulance—the baby is crowning. While Jack is in the ferryhouse, Dick drives off the ferry and into the adjacent parking lot. The baby is going to be born right there, by the slip.

Gabrielle Sophia Knight is caught either by her father or the future Edgartown police chief Paul Condlin; accounts vary. "For me, something beyond my thinking mind takes over," Daryl recalls of giving birth under these circumstances.

"I was stunned," agrees Dick. "It took me days to recover from that event."

A lighthearted tribute after the birth of Gabrielle Knight.

PAINTING BY JANIS LANGLEY

Among her skippers, the newly launched On Time II *quickly earns the nickname* Torpedo.

It doesn't. When launched at the far end of Katama Bay before a crowd of 150 on Sunday, October 26, 1969, the *On Time II* appears to levitate atop the water like a magic trick. The sides of her hull do not get wet. and the tips of her propellers show above the surface. When she runs, the props beat the water to a froth, with too much air rotating through the blades to start or stop the boat the way she must.

With a crew, and by hand, Jerry soon loads nine tons of concrete blocks—392 slabs of thirty-two pounds each, plus another 144 slabs of forty pounds each—into the bilge to weigh the ferry down to her proper waterline.

Now the *On Time II* floats where she should, but with all that extra weight, she is very hard to stop. Until they get the hang of it, her captains smash her into the slips, splintering bulkheads; crack into the ramps, buckling the pavement behind them; and crumple both ends of the ferry so badly they must each be rebuilt twice. Among her skippers, she quickly earns the nickname *Torpedo*.

But the trials of the new ferry, and her owner, are just beginning. The *On Time II* goes into service three months after an accident that—out of nowhere—draws the attention of the whole world to Chappaquiddick.

Overnight, "Chappaquiddick" becomes a morbid, transglobal byword for tragedy, mystery, and a dynastic curse.

On the evening of Friday, July 18, 1969—after racing in the Edgartown Yacht Club regatta all that day—Senator Edward M. Kennedy of Massachusetts hosts a party for twelve people, six men and six women, at a rented weekend cottage on Chappaquiddick. The women are all veterans of the presidential campaign of Robert F. Kennedy, which ends the year before with Robert's assassination in Los Angeles. The men are friends, employees, and relatives of Ted Kennedy.

Early the next morning, Mary Jo Kopechne, a twenty-eight-year-old staff member is found dead in a sedan belonging to Senator Kennedy, the car submerged upside down in the currents that race under the Dike Bridge into and out of Poucha Pond at the eastern end of the island.

Later that morning the senator tells the Edgartown police that he had been at the wheel, intending to take the young woman to the Chappy ferry just before midnight so that she could return to her hotel room in Edgartown, when he took a wrong turn down the Dike Road and drove off the bridge. But nine hours have passed since the accident occurred—a period when the young woman might have been saved and a fuller account of what happened established. The senator calls his own behavior inexcusable and later pleads guilty to leaving the scene of an accident after causing injury.

Overnight, "Chappaquiddick" becomes a morbid, transglobal byword for tragedy, mystery, and a dynastic curse.

"I just remember we went absolutely bonkers," says Jerry. "We had the *On Time I* on, and about three days after the Kennedy thing, I've forgotten what—something broke down on it. I had to wait for parts." With gawkers and the press queuing up in hordes, service depends for several days entirely upon a ferry designed to carry cars with spoked wheels and goo-gah horns. "So we were using the *City of Chappaquiddick*. And we were just trying to keep that thing together, because the new boat was still in my backyard. It was going to be launched that fall, luckily."

With gawkers and the press queuing up in hordes, service depends for several days entirely upon a ferry designed to carry cars with spoked wheels and goo-gah horns.

If there is one man who saves Chappaquiddick from being entirely overrun that summer, it is Jerry Grant, who resists all entreaties from journalists to run the ferry around the clock or let them bypass the car line.

"The reporters tried to buy me into going over at certain times," he remembers. "But I wouldn't do it. If I wasn't going to do it for the residents, I wasn't going to do it for them. We had hours and that's what we're going to run. I don't know whether it tripled that summer or not," says Jerry of the volume of cars and people. "But I know it was way beyond what we were capable of doing."

Fascination with the Dike Bridge endures that summer, the next, and the next. But once again visitors who come for one purpose take a moment to look around, and they discover the greater allure of Chappaquiddick: the long beaches and hilly trails, the shellfishing and surfcasting, the sense of remoteness and yet connectedness that the modern ferry offers.

Unlike the war or early years of the fishing derby, however, these newcomers discover Chappy by the thousands and all at once. On those summer days when even the *On Time II* can't keep up, Jerry runs the original *On Time* simultaneously to help clear away the backlog of cars. The two-ferry experiment works. Yet by the summer of 1974, it is clear to Jerry Grant that he is going to need a bigger boat.

As it happens, much of the financing for the newest ferry comes that year from Universal Studios, which chooses Martha's Vineyard to stand in for Amity, a fictional New England island menaced by a great white shark with a taste for human flesh.

By the summer of 1974, it is clear to Jerry Grant that he is going to need a bigger boat.

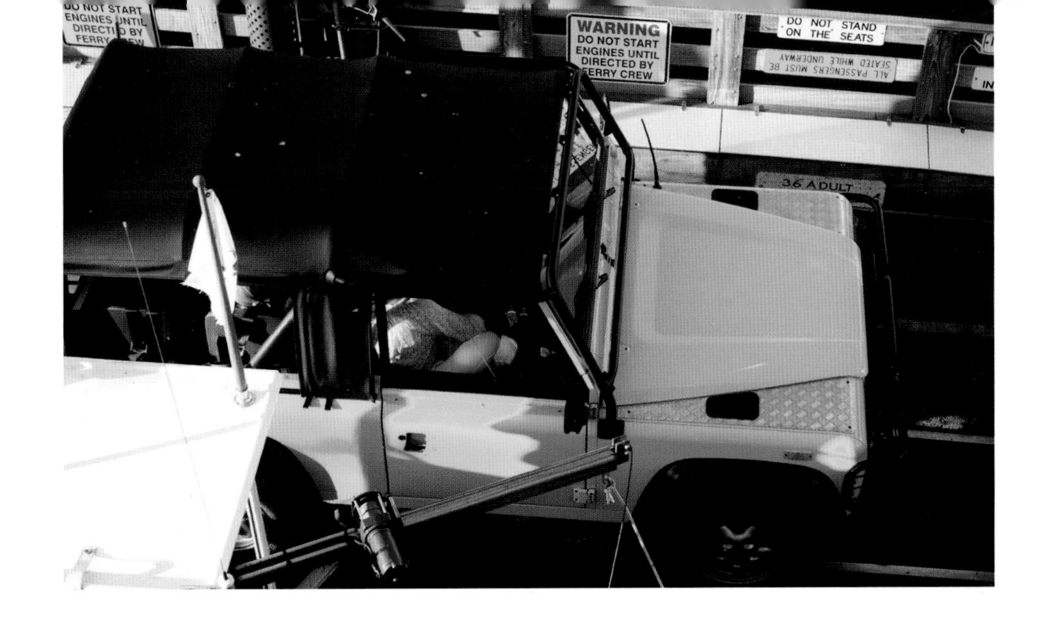

Director Steven Spielberg and co-screenwriter Carl Gottlieb stage a fateful scene on the deck of the first On Time.

From Grant and Carbon Marine—which Jerry also runs with a partner, Jack Carbon—the filmmakers rent workboats, cranes, and scows, including the *City of Chappaquiddick*, retired from ferry duties and now serving as a pier-building flatboat. Universal employs her as a self-propelled camera barge.

Director Steven Spielberg and co-screenwriter Carl Gottlieb also stage a two-minute scene on the deck of the first *On Time* in which the police chief, played by Roy Scheider, is persuaded against his better judgment to keep the beaches open after the first attack. "I did very well with them. I liked them," says Jerry. "I'd give them a bill on Thursdays, and on Fridays they'd put a check in my hand."

As *Jaws* wraps in the autumn of 1974 Jerry begins to think in detail about the second new ferry he plans to build. No marine architects this time, no new hull shapes—he will draw the *On Time III* himself and build only after he sees and feels the design at work.

NBC UNIVERSAL

Filming aboard the original *On Time*.

There is just one other ferry in the country whose routes, tides, and traffic approximate his own. In late November 1974 Jerry flies to Los Angeles with Jon Ahlbum, a marine mechanic, to look at the Balboa Island ferry, which Foster Silva and Richie Bettencourt skippered between the island and Balboa Peninsula in the 1950s and 1960s.

Jerry and Jon arrive to discover that one of the three Balboa ferries has been hauled onto a marine railway for their inspection. Because they sail in less current and flatter water, and carry more people but no heavy trucks, the Balboa ferries are lower in the water, narrower across the hull, but wider across the deck than the

BOTH PHOTOS: JERRY GRANT

En route to her launching, the *On Time III* turns onto Upper Main Street headed to Bend in the Road for her launch (right).

Sixty-four feet long, the On Time III *floats as she should, steams where she's pointed, and stops when she's asked.*

boat Jerry wants to build. Yet the Balboa model—particularly the form of the hull with its flat bottom and four parallel skegs—looks perfect. "They even let me run one out there," says Jerry. "I could feel the difference."

He launches his new ferry in early May 1975. Sixty-four feet long, the *On Time III* floats as she should, steams where she's pointed, and stops when she's asked. She goes to work only four weeks before the premiere of *Jaws*. Making her worldwide screen debut on June 20, 1975, the original *On Time* is first seen less than fifteen minutes into the film, plowing toward the Edgartown slip, the name *Amity* emblazoned across her bow.

It is the modern fate of Chappaquiddick and the ferry that things no longer happen in moderation around them. Just as the Dike Bridge accident turns out to be the most consequential car crash in American history, so *Jaws* turns out to be among the most consequential movies in Hollywood history—with compounding effects on the Vineyard, Chappy, and the ferry.

It helps that during this increasingly burdensome period, Jerry Grant employs several of the youngest captains and most energetic deckhands on record. Though mindful of their responsibilities, they bring a festive spirit to the ferry in harried times, occasionally heaving water balloons from one boat to the other and sometimes crossing close enough to exchange high-fives.

"I used to just show up in a bikini and sneakers," says Lucy Dahl, who starts work as a fifteen-year-old deckhand in 1981. "And also when it got hot, we'd jump in while the cars were coming in on Chappy. And I think that's why I loved it. There were no rules. As long as you showed up on time, and did your job, you could do what you want. You know how it is when you're on a sports team, and you really like everyone, and you're winning? That's kind of what it felt like."

Running in tandem during the busiest mornings and afternoons of the summer, the *On Time II* and *III* carry an average of a car a minute each way across the harbor. But Jerry Grant sometimes contends with lines a hundred yards long, running up Daggett Street and along Simpson's Lane, with two police officers managing a break in the queue at the intersections of North Water Street. To keep up with inflation, and with permission from the selectmen, he raises the rates four times during his twenty-two-year ownership.

Jerry also offers discounted tickets to Chappaquiddickers who live there all year. But the requirement of proof strikes full-time residents as intrusive, and being left out strikes seasonal residents as unfair. Some Chappaquiddickers want the ferry to run more often during winter evenings, and some feel the town should now own or subsidize it, entirely or in part.

Jerry wearies of the conflicts: He is a workingman who has held down costs and fares by building his own boats for much less than a shipyard would charge. He believes he oversees a responsive operation with no bureaucracy and little overhead. And he feels he never earns what a private owner running an essential public service should.

"I made good money to live on," says Jerry, "but I never made the kind of money you should be putting aside as a business."

The most eventful period in the history of the Chappy ferry—quite possibly the most eventful in the history of any ferry anywhere—ends the last week of January 1988, when Jerry Grant sells it to Roy Hayes and the one person who knows the business as well as he does: his daughter Debbie Grant.

Former deckhand Lucy Dahl in the summer of 2011 with 1981 journal entry.

Ferry Schedule, 1979

- Off-season: 7:30 a.m.–6 p.m., 7:00–7:15 p.m., 9:00–9:30 p.m., 11:00–11:15 p.m.
- Summer: 7:30 a.m.–midnight
- On call after scheduled hours

Fares

- 1968 (each way): passenger: $.15; car and driver: $.75 ($.98 and $4.88 in 2012 dollars, respectively)
- 1976 (each way): passenger: $.20; car and driver: $1.00 ($.80 and $3.98 in 2012 dollars, respectively)
- 1979 (each way): passenger: $.25; car and driver: $1.25 ($.78 and $3.90 in 2012 dollars, respectively)
- 1986 (each way): passenger: $.35; car and driver: $1.75 ($.72 and $3.62 in 2012 dollars, respectively)

Population on Chappaquiddick

- 1970: Fifteen estimated, year-round
- 1972: Thirty-two year-round
- 1973: Forty-nine year-round

"Okay, you can take us back now."

It is a fateful scene in the movie, the one in which the chief of police, Martin Brody (Roy Scheider), reluctantly agrees to keep the beaches of Amity Island open after the first shark attack the night before. "It's all psychological," the mayor (Murray Hamilton) warns him. "You yell 'barracuda,' everybody says, 'Huh? What?' You yell 'shark'—and we've got a panic on our hands on the Fourth of July."

As they explore the Vineyard in the winter of 1974, Joe Alves, the production designer of *Jaws*, and Bill Gilmore, the production executive, draw up a list of locations that would bring the fictional Amity Island to dramatic life. In the *On Time* scene, Boy Scouts are on a mile swim to earn their merit badges the morning after the first attack.

"The best way to put the principals in proximity to the kids would be on the ferry," says Carl Gottlieb, the screenwriter with Peter Benchley and the actor who plays *Amity Gazette* editor Larry Meadows. "Everything was working for it—picturesque location, logistics, you could see the Boy Scouts in the water in the background. And on the ferry, you got the benefits of movement, action, water—all the elements were present."

One challenge is that the real ferry service must carry on while the scene is shot; in the background, the *On Time II* crosses the other way doing her regular job as the older ferry does her cinematic one.

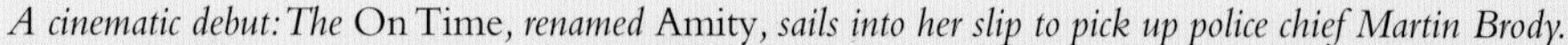

A cinematic debut: The On Time, *renamed* Amity, *sails into her slip to pick up police chief Martin Brody.*

NBC UNIVERSAL

ALL PHOTOS ON THIS PAGE EDITH BLAKE/COURTESY MARTHAS VINEYARD MUSEUM

Above and inset: Filming a sinking Orca *from the camera barge* City of Chappaquiddick.

"The great thing about the ferryboat is that you have a limited choice of angles, and the audience accepts that, because they know we're on a small craft," says Carl. The whole scene plays out in one trip and two shots, and neither the ferry nor the chief finish the journey they intend to make. The mayor orders the captain, Dick Hewitt, to take them back before they land. "For Brody," says Carl, "it's a turning point he regrets making."

Much less heralded is the role of the *City of Chappaquiddick*.

Painted army green and thoroughly battered as she nears age forty, the old ferry works as a pier-building scow for Grant and Carbon Marine. Jerry Grant leases her to Universal Studios that summer, along with other floating equipment, and he believes that her role as a camera barge may be the last commercial job she ever does. With her wide, flat deck, she serves as the perfect platform from which to film the final confrontation with the marauding shark, much of it shot in the shallows of Katama Bay.

The two newest ferries make cameos in two sequels, *Jaws 2* and *Jaws: The Revenge.* In this final film, the *On Time II* veers away from her regular route and sails beyond the lighthouse with a taxicab and Brody family aboard. There are more inexplicable sequences in the fourth *Jaws* movie than this.

But not many.

Shooting Jaws *may be the final job the* City of Chappaquiddick *ever does.*

CHAPTER 11

Debra J. Grant and Roy M. Hayes
1988–1998
Roy M. Hayes
1998–2008

Debbie Grant is six years old when her dad, Jerry Grant, comes home one early spring night in 1966 with the news that he has bought the Chappaquiddick ferry. With this announcement, the Grant family begins an association with the ferry that will last for thirty-two years, second in length only to Charlie Osborn, whose tenure ends almost a half-century earlier.

"I didn't remember my father ever really being involved in boats," says Debbie. The night he buys the business, Jerry takes her down to the Edgartown slip on his scooter to see what the family has taken on. "I remember that there wasn't any fence there. We pulled into the parking lot at the ferry, and I thought we were going to go over the edge," she says.

Among her favorite memories from girlhood are the nights when Jerry sits his children down at the dining room table and makes them count the change the ferry has earned that day. "Count the quarters in piles of four, the dimes in piles of ten, stack the pennies up, count them out in rows, put them in wrappers," Debbie says. "He would be so clear: 'Do not drop any money, don't take any of it, be careful with what you're doing—this is very serious!' The next day we would always find money under the radiator, even though none of us ever dropped any, and he let us keep the money that we found. It didn't occur to me until I was an adult that he put the money under the radiator as our pay for working."

Debbie Grant and her father, Jerry Grant.

Debra J. Grant is born February 5, 1960, the daughter of Dorothy Lima Grant and Jerry Grant. With her brother and sisters, she works as a deckhand during the hectic but jubilant period when the young crews high-five each other as the ferries cross, leave teasing notes for the other boat on the ramps, and dive in between trips.

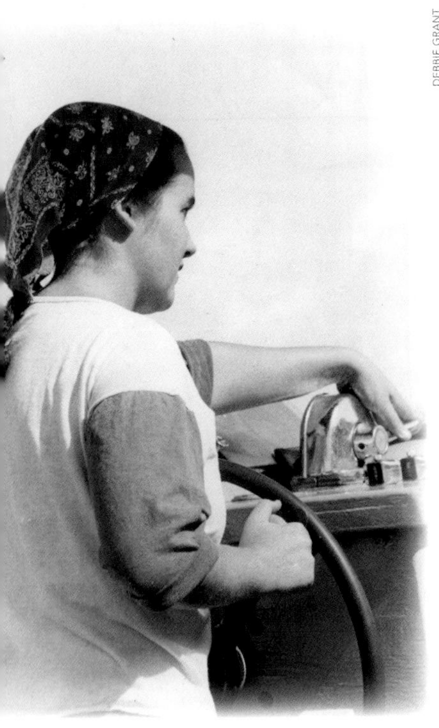
DEBBIE GRANT

Debbie Grant at the wheel.

On Tuesday, July 29, 1980, Debbie herself makes history when she becomes the first licensed woman to skipper the ferry across the channel. But the lack of enlightenment among the traveling public astonishes her: "Constant remarks about being a woman driver, constantly, all day long," she remembers. Debbie has a talent for taking pictures, especially landscapes and faces, and she studies photography in college and graduate school. But in 1982 she returns to the Island to manage the ferry for her father and drive the boats.

Debbie Grant does not know it yet, but she is now on course to meet the man she will marry. In partnership with him, the first woman to skipper the Chappaquiddick ferry will also become the first woman to own it.

Roy M. Hayes is born July 20, 1945, in the Bronx. His father, Roy J. Hayes, is a motorman on the Third Avenue elevated railway, and his mother, Anne, is a homemaker. Roy leaves home at eighteen and works at a remarkable array of jobs—in a boatyard, repairing and restoring sports and antique cars, running the cameras and setting off explosives for a submersible six thousand fathoms down in the Philippine Trench, and serving as foreman at a scenery shop in New York City. In 1969 he moves to the Vineyard, where he helps to construct the Black Dog Tavern in Vineyard Haven, builds and restores houses, and makes cabinets.

On Tuesday, July 29, 1980, Debbie Grant makes history when she becomes the first licensed woman to skipper the ferry across the channel.

Those who command sometimes also crew: Debbie Grant takes tickets as a deckhand.

DEBBIE GRANT

At the Helm: Tara J. Whiting

Her great-great-grandfather Henry L. Whiting was one of the notable cartographers of the nineteenth century, surveying sections of the American coastline from New Orleans to the Canadian border. She lives in the farmhouse Henry bought in 1852. She is a horsewoman, West Tisbury town clerk, and devotee of the *Star Wars* films.

So how does Tara J. Whiting become the only captain to serve on the Chappy ferry from the western Vineyard countryside? Through family: Debbie Grant is a down-Island cousin, and Tara begins to work as a deckhand in May 1994. She gets her license a year later.

Like Debbie—but unlike nearly all the men who captain the ferry—the *On Time II* is her favorite boat. "She's predictable in her unpredictability," says Tara. "There's something about not quite knowing what's going to happen with her that is wonderfully consistent."

He also abuses drugs and alcohol, almost at the cost of his life, but he is nearly two and a half years sober when he meets Debbie Grant. Just before they marry in 1988, they buy the ferry from her father for $750,000 over ten years (about $1.44 million in 2011).

The town "knew my past, my history on the Vineyard, they trusted Jerry, and they let me do it," says Roy. "People looked at you here like this: If you had ability, they were willing to forgive and help you. That wasn't true where I came from. Here it was much more of a personable community. And that was very important."

For her part, Debbie is at first reluctant to buy the service. From long experience, she knows that it is a full-time job and twenty-four-hour worry. But she already knows how to run the operation, and Roy has the skills to look after the boats. She comes to welcome the chance to take over a business she has long managed for her father.

DEBBIE GRANT

Debbie Grant and Roy Hayes

It is clear from the start of the ownership of Debbie and Roy that the press of cars and trucks trying to cross the harbor in summer is often beyond what even two ferries can keep up with.

For Roy, the challenge is different. "First, it's fear," he says. "And then it was me delving into the mechanics of the ferry, and learning it, and repairing it as it was, and then looking for ways to improve things, and earning the respect of the Chappy people. I looked on it as a tremendous responsibility."

It is clear from the start of the ownership of Debbie and Roy that the press of cars and trucks trying to cross the harbor in summer is often beyond what even two ferries can keep up with.

There are mornings when it takes a supervisor and four police officers to manage the line in Edgartown, and they sometimes tell new arrivals to come back later when the line reaches the intersection of Simpson's Lane and Pease's Point Way, nearly a quarter of a mile from the landing. In the afternoons on Chappy, the line stretches the same distance to the beach club or beyond. Waits can last up to an hour on either side.

It also becomes plain during the Grant and Hayes era that the ferry has adapted and grown almost as much as it can: Because the distance is so short and the boating traffic so heavy, there can be no third ferry on the route. Because of the size and design of the slips, the strength of the currents, and expense of larger crews, the boats cannot easily be much longer or wider. Because there are few if any other places to build roads and slips on either side of the harbor, the ferry cannot change where it lands.

And because Chappy would declare war, there cannot be a bridge.

A Beach Torn Open, a Ferry Route Reconfigured

In the darkness of early morning, April 17, 2007—during what comes to be called the Patriots' Day Storm—the abrasive forces of gale winds and storm tides overwhelm the sands of South Beach. That night, Katama Bay bursts through the beach to the Atlantic. For the first time since the winter of 1977, Chappaquiddick is separated from the rest of the Vineyard in fact as well as name.

For those who have never seen what happens when Edgartown Harbor is suddenly opened to the ocean at the southern end as well as through the regular entrance at the northern end, the effects are extraordinary.

The tides tumble through the harbor all day and night with the force of a flash flood. Currents whirlpool around piers, form rips in the middle of the channel, reverse direction unpredictably, shovel channel buoys onto their sides, rush over mooring balls, and compel yachts to sail backward even as they try to drive forward with their sails full.

The bullying current is strongest at the harbor entrance, where the tides now sweep the ferries in great parabolic arcs up and down the harbor as they try to cross. Sometimes the rush of water carries them three hundred feet south of the opposite slip, more than half the distance across. The sailing time often doubles as the ferries fight their way upstream, waves pounding against their bows, before they finally turn and shoulder their way heavily into a slip.

"The most incredible feeling," Brad Fligor, a skipper, tells *Martha's Vineyard Magazine* a few years later, "was coming from Chappy to the Edgartown side, getting swept down toward the end of Memorial Wharf, and having to make my way back up so I could get into the Edgartown slip. And being full throttle and looking to the port side, parallel to Memorial Wharf, and really not going anywhere. I mean, I'm full steam, coming up so that I can make a turn into the slip, and just barely, barely inching forward."

MICHAEL BERWIND

ROY HAYES

Installing a new ramp at the Edgartown slip, 1994.

"That filled a big hole in my life. My life was the ferry," says Roy Hayes. "Whatever I did, wherever I went, the ferry was always there. It's like your heart beating, the basis of everything you do every day."

Chappaquiddick is small and separate, so the consequences of change appear starkly and immediately, foreshadowing where the Vineyard may be heading as a whole. There are more than four hundred houses on Chappy at the start of the Roy and Debbie period; with the minimum lot size now zoned for three acres, and the town issuing new building permits at an average rate of eight per year through most of the 1990s, it is possible to envision the day when there will be no more land on which to build.

In the meantime, as newcomers construct and expand their houses, many long-time Chappy residents worry about losing a common, unspoken understanding of what the little island has been in the past, is today, and should be as time goes on.

"I have asked people on Chappaquiddick what I should do," says Roy in 1998. "The most they want me to do is nothing. They don't want me to lengthen the boats, add more boats, or run longer hours. They don't want me to increase the service. They don't want to make Chappy any more desirable."

By default, traffic management falls to the ferry, its owners, and a weirdly oxymoronic philosophy—but still a plausibly effective one: The longer the lines to Chappaquiddick, goes this idea, the less people will want to make the trip. The service that transports visitors also stops some of them from coming. More crowds equals crowd control.

As the pressures of growth on Chappy rise, Edgartown remains as hesitant as ever to support a ferry that runs entirely within its own boundaries. It owns the slips and ferryhouses, but in the spring of 1990, on the floor of the town meeting, voters decline to override a statewide cap on taxes and appropriate three hundred thousand dollars to rebuild the ramps, which the town also owns.

Fearing a calamity on Chappy should a ramp fail, thereby preventing an emergency vehicle from going across, Roy, Debbie, and the town win passage of a state law allowing Edgartown to lease the ferryhouses, slips, and ramps to the owners, who become entirely responsible for their maintenance. Roy and a crew replace both ramps in the spring of 1994.

The result is that, apart from licensing the owner and setting the maximum rates, Edgartown bears hardly any more overarching responsibility for the Chappy ferry at the end of its second century of operation than when Uriah Morse pulls on his oars in the age of whaling and evangelism. The ferry sails on as it almost always has:

a public service run by a private owner, supported not by the town but only by its users, central to the lives of residents living on one side of the harbor but peripheral to most of those living on the other.

Debbie Grant and Roy Hayes divorce in 1998, and Roy buys Debbie's half of the ferry. It is hard for Debbie to let go of a service that has been in the Grant family for more than three decades. But she returns to her life as a photographer; marries Michael Cassidy, a painting contractor; has her third child; resumes her studies in education; and begins to work as an assistant teacher at the Edgartown School.

As sole owner, Roy replaces the engines in both boats and converts them to hydraulic drive, the big steering wheels giving way to tiny electric toggles. He marries Lisa Burke, who as Lisa Hayes years later will run the Animal Shelter of Martha's Vineyard; they have six children from previous marriages. In 2007 Roy begins to think about selling the ferry. He worries about liability in an age of lawsuits, and he believes that the service may now be too much for a private owner to handle.

Even so, at the end of his tenure, he reflects on what ownership means to him.

"That filled a big hole in my life. My life was the ferry," he says. "Whatever I did, wherever I went, the ferry was always there. It's like your heart beating, the basis of everything you do every day."

Illustration of the *On Time III* showing Roy Hayes' truck at the bow, a wedding gift to him from his captains and deckhands.

ILLUSTRATION: DANA GAINES / COURTESY ROY HAYES

Ferry Schedule, 2007

- Off-season: 7:30 a.m.–6 p.m., 7:00–7:15 p.m., 9:00–9:30 p.m., 11:00–11:15 p.m.
- Summer: 7:30 a.m.–midnight
- On call after scheduled hours

Fares

- 1990 (each way): passenger: $.50; car and driver: $2.00 ($.87 and $3.46 in 2012 dollars, respectively)
- 1996 (each way): passenger: $.50; car and driver: $2.50 ($.72 and $3.61 in 2012 dollars, respectively)
- 2000 (each way): passenger: $.75; car and driver: $3.00 ($.99 and $3.94 in 2012 dollars, respectively)
- 2002 (each way): passenger: $1.00; car and driver: $4.00 ($1.26 and $5.03 in 2012 dollars, respectively)
- 2004 (each way): passenger $1.50; car and driver: $5.00 ($1.80 and $5.99 in 2012)

Population on Chappaquiddick

- 1990: 112 year-round, estimated
- 2001: 125 year-round, estimated

STOP
NO PASSENGERS BEYOND THIS POINT
WARNING
KEEP HANDS INSIDE OF RAILS
FIRE EQUIPMENT
STOP
NO PASSENGERS BEYOND THIS POINT
KEEP HANDS INSIDE OF RAILS
NO SMOKING
DO NOT STAND ON THE SEATS
ALL PASSENGERS MUST BE SEATED WHILE UNDERWAY
20 ADULT LIFE PRESERVERS

CHAPTER 12

Peter S. Wells and Sally T. Snipes

2008–Present

When Roy Hayes sells the ferry to Peter Wells and his wife, Sally Snipes, at the end of January 2008, it feels to some who know Peter as if an old, half-forgotten waterfront prophecy has just been fulfilled.

It's not just that Peter is the longest-serving employee of the ferry, going back to boyhood days as a deckhand in the early 1960s. Nor is it the fact that, for the first time since the era of Foster Silva fifty-five years before, the ferry once again belongs to a couple who actually lives on Chappy.

For though Peter Wells has left the ferry service a number of times during his long career as a crew member and captain—each time apparently for good—what his friends, colleagues, and several generations of ferry passengers take note of is how many times he has come back to it.

As a boy on Chappaquiddick, Peter larks about with friends on land and water as any kid would, but there are home movies of him and his chums paddling around in a plywood mockup of the *On Time* in Katama Bay, and his mother, Polly, remembers him hanging around the Chappy slip a good deal as a lad. It is fair to suggest that, however indirect his course to ownership may have run, it begins quite early in his life.

Sally Snipes and Peter Wells, summer of 2011.

Below: Peter (center) and family members during his earliest years on Chappaquiddick.
Left: Peter's son-in-law Erik Gilley, mechanic, welder, scuba diver, and all around fixer.

PETER WELLS AND SALLY SNIPES

PETER WELLS AND SALLY SNIPES

Peter Wells skippers the Edgartown Yacht Club launch, middle 1970s.

Russell Wells, Peter's father, serves as a fighter pilot in Italy during World War II. He marries Polly in Hawaii in 1947, and Peter, born March 21, 1952, is the third child and first son of their five children. The family moves all over the country because of Russell's service in the air force. He retires as a major and goes to work as a pilot for National Executive Airlines in New England and in the Southeast.

The Wells family spends summers on Chappaquiddick until January 1964, when Russell dies in a plane crash flying for the airline in Stuart, Florida. Polly and the family are living in Edgartown, and after Russell's death, she buys a house in town, where Peter attends sixth through ninth grades. The Wells family then moves back to its last mainland home in Chatham Township, New Jersey.

Peter loves ships and sailing, and he graduates from Maine Maritime Academy in the spring of 1974, twenty-two years old and newly married to Jeanne Boober of Castine, Maine. Peter might have gone to sea, but the young couple is expecting a child, and they move to Chappy, which feels like home to Peter and a place where he has the best chance to land a good job.

On his first day back, he crosses to town to check the help-wanted pages in the *Vineyard Gazette*. Jerry Grant is skippering the ferry. "I only had a dime to buy the paper, or whatever the price was," recalls Peter. "Jerry said, 'Hey, don't you have a license to drive these boats?' I said, 'Sure.' So the next day I was driving the boat—captain of the vessel from the first day on the job. You can't beat that."

"So the next day I was driving the boat," says Peter, "captain of the vessel from the first day on the job. You can't beat that."

Peter also works at Pimpneymouse Farm, owned for many years by Edith and Robert Potter. He plows fields, plants seed, and cuts hay. Peter and Jeanne separate, and Peter becomes a young single father to his nineteen-month-old daughter, Nearess. He needs someone to look after his little girl while he works, so in the fall of 1976 Peter takes her to the family day-care program Sally Snipes runs in Oak Bluffs. He falls for Sally right away, and he begins to bring food and make things for the children in her charge.

"He courted me with goat's milk and carob-coated pineapple," says Sally. "And he made the most beautiful little darling slide for my little kids. And put up swings. He could do everything. He made going to the dump fun. Just everything was fun with Peter."

A Nightmare Come to Life

Peter and Sally Snipes have owned the ferry for two months when, a little after eleven o'clock on the night of Thursday, March 27, 2008, a Mercedes hybrid sport utility vehicle rolls forward as the ferry slows in the Chappy slip, breaks through the chain, and sinks.

All three occupants—the driver, her daughter, and her daughter's boyfriend—exit the car before it goes under. Captain Brad Fligor and the boyfriend pull the two women on deck without serious injuries.

The police report says the driver, a woman from Pennsylvania, is pretending to drive the ferry by turning the steering wheel back and forth as the ferry lands, with the engine still running. Afterward, the car is dragged ashore by a towboat and a wrecker.

Police charge the driver with negligent operation of an automobile and operating under the influence of alcohol, and the captain and ferry are absolved of blame. "I've seen this one a thousand times before in my nightmares," says Peter, relieved after it's all over.

Born October 10, 1952, Sally T. Snipes grows up the second of six children on a hundred-acre family farm in Bucks County, Pennsylvania. Her father, Samuel, is an attorney; her mother, Barbara, a homemaker and volunteer. The family is Quaker.

Sally spends the fall of 1974 on the Vineyard as a student teacher. After graduating from Wheelock College in 1975 with a bachelor of science degree in early childhood education, she returns to the Island and, under the guidance of Helen Maley of Martha's Vineyard Community Services, opens a family day care program, where she soon meets Peter and Nearess.

With their two young daughters, they move in before the new home is finished.

Peter and Sally live in a tent in the woods for the summer, close enough for Peter to bike to the ferry. A daughter, Molly, is born the following spring. Sally's father buys the family land on Chappy, and Peter begins to build a house. With their two young daughters, they move in before the home is finished.

"We had no car, no running water, no electricity," says Sally. "I either burned the food or it took forever to cook on the wood stove. I was wretched. And the mud! The mud was just everywhere."

Dressing Up—or Down—Depending on the Job

Not since the era of Jimmy Yates has a skipper of the Chappy ferry taken such care to dress the part. Matt Wetzel, at twenty, is the youngest summertime captain on the line, and when needed he works as a deckhand instead. As a deckhand he wears a proletarian T-shirt with his name and "Ferry Crew" Magic Markered on the back. As captain, he wears a white shirt, epaulets with four bars, and anchor pins. "I've had people ask my deckhands whether this is a joke, or am I serious about this," says Matt, who takes in every reaction with a smile. "I like the way it adds a bit of professionalism to the job."

MARK ALAN LOVEWELL

After a winter refit, the *On Time III* departs Vineyard Haven as the Steamship Authority ferry *Martha's Vineyard* arrives from Woods Hole, January 2012.

To try something new, Peter steps down as a full-time captain and begins work as a surveyor for Glenn Provost of Vineyard Land Surveying in 1986. With his history on the ferry reaching back to his boyhood more than twenty years before, it is hard for Peter to leave—and indeed, even as a surveyor he continues to keep a hand in, skippering the ferry on weekends.

"Peter has always loved the ferry, from the time he was a little boy," says Sally. "He just loves the *boats*. He loves the workings of the boats. He loves the hum of those engines. He never really stopped working on it. Sometimes on his way home, he would finish out Roy's shift just to be on the ferry."

"Peter has always loved the ferry, from the time he was a little boy," says Sally. "He just loves the boats*."*

Roy Hayes's decision to sell the business in the spring of 2007 comes exactly two hundred years after the first record of the existence of a Chappaquiddick ferry. Chappy, of course, is an island entirely transformed—by notoriety, by fame, and by the enchantment of its own rough and isolated beauty.

Up, Up, and Away: The Mystic Sport of Aqua-Biking

Peter Wells spends a good deal of time these days thinking about the safety of the whole ferry operation. That's why it's so ironic that it should have been Peter and his younger brother-in-law, Ran Snipes, who in the summer of 1979 invent the sport of aqua-biking.

Ran is nineteen and visiting Peter and Sally that summer when he looks around one day and asks, "Why can't we ride a bike into the water? Can't we just ride off a pier?" Though he himself is twenty-seven years old, Peter has never quite shaken a boyhood love for pulling stunts on the water.

Ran and Peter conduct the first in a series of bike-to-water experiments along the Chappy harborfront—off a pier without a ramp, then off a pier with one. Neither gives them the height or distance they require. Peter thinks this over. Suddenly it occurs to him:

Chappy ferry! I'm friends with those guys. I just drove the ferry this afternoon. They're not going to tell me to stop.

In those days there is no gate at the ramp, so Ran and Peter find a used-up ten-speed, lock it in the highest gear, tie an empty milk jug to the back, and on an afternoon when there is little traffic, they take aim from the fourth pole on the Chappy Road. As soon as the ferry leaves the slip, a colleague raises the ramp high.

"When you saw the ramp going up," says Peter, "you'd go careening down there and fly off into the slip." Bike and rider hit the water with the splash of a depth charge. The rider surfaces and swims the jug to the ramp. The colleague hauls up rider and bike—and after the next suitable departure of the ferry, they do it again.

That summer, Woody Filley and his brother, Jonathan, film a leap in which Peter and bike almost clear the end of the slip. "And that was the longest jump I ever made," says Peter. "I smacked my butt, really smacked it hard."

To add a sense of drama to the escapade, Peter soon arranges for Jack Carbon, a captain, to begin pulling out from the slip as Peter rockets down the road on his bike, crying out for the ferry to stop. Alarmed, passengers try to persuade Jack to return, but he brushes them off. The last thing they see is Peter Wells flying toward them, bug-eyed and open-mouthed—and literally falling a few feet short.

Thus Chappaquiddickers continue to worry about the pace and scale of construction, the length of the automobile lines in summer, and the recent rise in fares as the ferry begins its third century of operation. But what causes Edgartown officials and Chappy residents to ask urgent questions about who should run it, and how it should be supported, comes as a sudden and complete surprise.

The surprise is the Patriots' Day Storm of 2007.

For three days in the middle of April of that year, a gale with gusts thundering over sixty knots claws and tears at the Vineyard shoreline from the southeast. A few hours after midnight on April 17, wind and tide conspire to blow an opening through South Beach, separating Chappaquiddick from the rest of Martha's Vineyard for the first time since early 1977.

For the past thirty years it has been possible for those with four-wheel-drive vehicles to avoid the ferry, if they choose, by driving across the beach from Chappy to the main Island and back.

But the severing of South Beach means there is no longer any way to cross by car or truck except by ferry—and that there may not be an alternative for another fifteen or twenty years, if the new opening lasts as long as previous openings have. It is the prospect of nearly total dependence on the ferry for a generation to come that spurs Edgartown and Chappy to ask about fares, car lines, and ownership in the years ahead.

The prospect of near total dependence on the ferry for a generation to come spurs Edgartown and Chappy to ask new questions about the future of the service.

Among Chappy residents there is general relief that the ferry is now in the hands of neighbors they know well.

That spring, Edgartown selectmen appoint a committee of eleven Chappaquiddickers to study the service and advise whether the town should buy it. In the fall the committee files a detailed but inconclusive report recommending against either town or private ownership, suggesting in the interim that a new committee counsel the town on ferry issues.

But then something very much in the lifelong, improvisational, path-of-least-resistance spirit of the ferry occurs: Roy Hayes simply offers it to Peter and Sally for $3.3 million. They agree, the selectmen approve a transfer of the license, and on January 22, 2008, Peter Wells and Sally Snipes become the eleventh known owners of the Chappaquiddick ferry.

Among Chappy residents there is general relief that, for all the analysis just given to the question of ownership, the ferry is now in the hands of neighbors they know well.

Peter is captain of the Chappaquiddick fire company and an emergency medical technician. Sally has been a massage therapist and nursery school teacher. But with automobile fares, adjusted for inflation, higher than at any time since the first years of Tony Bettencourt's ownership, and passenger fares the highest ever, there is also amazement on Chappy at the price the ferry commands.

Roy says that there are others—individuals, boatyards, ferry companies—who are prepared to pay what he asks. But Roy chooses Peter and Sally because Peter is a Chappaquiddicker, and because "he really wanted it and had worked for me for twenty years. And he was comfortable on the water."

PETER WELLS AND SALLY SNIPES

A younger Peter Wells with Chappaquiddick fire truck.

After the sale, Roy returns to cabinetmaking and woodworking. For the first time in a generation, he can drive beyond the perimeter of the town without worrying about a ferry breaking down, and he can sleep through the night without wondering whether he will wake to a call for an ambulance, police, or more fire trucks on Chappy.

Peter is recently retired from his surveying job when he and Sally buy the service. For him, ownership means that fellow Chappaquiddickers will never have to worry whether a faraway agency or business is looking after the ferry as it should. No one else, he

At the Helm: Captains Charlie Ross and Brad Fligor

Charlie Ross and Brad Fligor, both of Edgartown, are the senior captains of the Chappy ferry and have each served at least twenty-five years. In that quarter century, Peter Wells believes each captain has, at the very least:

- Made over a quarter of a million round-trips.
- Traveled over fifty thousand miles back and forth (more than one-fifth of the distance to the moon).
- Walked over thirteen thousand miles on deck (more than halfway around the world at the equator).
- Spent almost forty-six thousand hours aboard (about five years).
- Carried over 1 million cars.
- Carried over 2 million passengers.

Brad Fligor (left) and Charlie Ross

reasons, will maintain and repair the boats as effectively as he will. No one else will make sure the profits go back into the service.

"I didn't wake up one morning twenty-five years ago and say, 'I'm going to own that ferry some day!'" says Peter. He recalls his previous resignations from the service to avoid the pressure of summertime traffic, or to work full-time as a surveyor, or to move—albeit briefly—to the mainland. "There have been at least half a dozen times when I got off the ferry and said, 'Well, that's the last time I'm ever going to drive this boat. I'm going to miss this. This is the end of an era for me.'"

Peter agrees he may have been fated to own the ferry all along. "You know," he says, "all of these things that have happened in my life made it possible for this *to happen."*

But looking back over his time on Chappaquiddick, his studies at Maine Maritime, and his career running the boats, Peter agrees that he may have been fated to own the ferry all along. "You know," he says, "all of these things that have happened in my life made it possible for *this* to happen."

Water Music—and Other Festivities on the Chappaquiddick Ferry

In the summers of 2010 and 2011, the West Tisbury Congregational Church Bell Choir plays a series of sundown concerts from the deck of the *On Time II* as she slowly sails among the boats and boaters moored in Edgartown Harbor, who can't quite believe what they're seeing and hearing as the ferry glides by them. Peter Wells and Sally Snipes hope the addition of a third boat will allow them to offer cruise parties for weddings, picnickers, and harbor tourists—and anyone else who hankers to take the ferry not just back and forth, but all around.

For Sally, the decision to buy is harder. She does not share Peter's love of commercial vessels. She worries about how ownership may change her relationship with friends on Chappy. She worries about stress and costs and income.

What makes it all much easier is that daughter, Molly, and son-in-law, Erik Gilley, move from Cape Cod to Chappy with their three toddler daughters so that Molly can help with the business and Erik can oversee the maintenance of the ferries. Keeping up the recent tradition, the Chappy ferry again becomes a family affair.

When Peter and Sally assume ownership, the *On Time II* is nearing thirty-nine years of age, the *On Time III* approaching thirty-three. Both have served longer than any Chappy ferry in the twentieth century—and quite possibly ever.

They are also the hardest-working commercial boats to be found anywhere along the coastline of Martha's Vineyard. The loads they carry are often brutishly heavy, the route they sail short and mechanically punishing. Near the end of his ownership, Roy Hayes reasons that both ferries may be nearing the ends of their useful lives, and he draws plans for two new boats, which will look and run much like the *On Time III*.

But Peter believes that the sister ferries can serve forever if looked after meticulously, and he begins a program to refit the hulls, mechanics, electrical systems, and hydraulics of both boats.

In 2010 Peter, Erik, and captains George Fisher, Jonathan Morse, and Jeff LaMarche replace three-quarters of the frames in the hull of the *On Time II*, rebuild and re-fiberglass her deck, reconstruct her captain's console, reconfigure her propeller shafts, and rewire the hull; she is also given a new engine in the summer.

In 2011 they also begin to refit the *On Time III*, replacing deck frames under the pilot house, rebuilding the watertight bulkheads and a quarter of the deck, and replacing mechanical gear below the waterline both inside and outside the hull.

In fact, Peter and Sally begin to think not only of the length of time the two ferries may eventually run, but also of the generations that may own them later on. Molly and Erik Gilley work for the ferry today, and five grandchildren are coming along who could each serve as deckhands in the next ten or fifteen years. One or more might one day grow up to own and run the Chappy ferry themselves.

"I could see it being in my family for years and years to come," says Peter. "There's no reason to let it go. I love boats, and I know ferries." He recalls the options he faced when he graduated from Maine Maritime. "I didn't want to go to sea. I had been to sea as a midshipman, and I knew that I wanted to be home at night." He thinks a moment about all the things that once drew him away from a service that, fatefully or not, he now expects to run for the rest of his life.

"I like ferries," Peter says with a smile. "They're the way to go."

Ferry Schedule, 2008–present

- Off-season: 6:45 a.m.–7:30 p.m., 9:00 p.m.–10:00 p.m., 11:00 p.m.–11:15 p.m.
- May 26–October 15: 6:45 a.m.–midnight
- On call for emergencies

Fares, 2008–present

- Passenger: $2.00 each way
- Car and driver: $6.00 each way

Population on Chappaquiddick, 2011

- 135 year-round, estimated

Captain George Fisher works aboard the *On Time III* during the overhaul beginning in October 2011. Temporary housing shields the workers.

AFTERWORD

The Ferry in the Future

WHAT WAS TRUE OF THE CHAPPY FERRY TWENTY-FIVE YEARS AGO, WHEN THE CAR LINES FIRST BEGAN to challenge the *On Time II* and *III* even as the boats ran in tandem on summer mornings and afternoons, is true today and will assuredly remain true tomorrow:

There is little or no room to run more or larger boats across the harbor entrance. Nor is it possible to move the landings of the service anywhere else on either side. Nor can the ferry accommodate the heaviest traffic in any way other than to ask for patience from those who are willing to bear with it.

In the winter of 2012, as this book goes to press, Peter Wells and Sally Snipes are in fact preparing to build a third ferry for the service. Not to run back and forth in company with the existing boats, but to ensure that there are always two ferries in the water, ready to work all year round, when a third boat breaks down in summer or is hauled onto a railway for maintenance in the off-season.

The addition of a third ferry will mark the greatest advance in the operation since the launch of the *On Time II*, which began crossing the harbor entrance without having to turn around in 1969, and the *On Time III*, which doubled the number of cars that the ferries could manage beginning in 1975.

But Peter and Sally are considering an innovation that would make the new ferry as noteworthy a vessel as Tony Bettencourt's motorized scow of 1935. The hull would be of steel, because today it can be less expensive to build with steel than with wood and fiberglass, as the two *On Time* ferries were. And Peter and his crew can more easily maintain and repair a steel hull over time.

Even more pioneering, assuming reliable, rechargeable lithium ion batteries can be found: the new ferry would be driven not by a diesel engine but by an electric motor.

"I feel if it's anywhere near what it costs to run a diesel, that's fine," says Peter. "The boat will be quieter. It'll be cleaner. It will be ahead of the curve when it comes to meeting new EPA regulations, which get stiffer all the time. And I just think it would be nice if, every time the boat sets out, it didn't make a loud rumbling noise and smoke didn't belch out of the stack. I think that would be neat."

There can be only one name for a boat as farsighted as this one might turn out to be, and to honor the time when Tony Bettencourt dreamed up a new type of ferry for the service. Peter and Sally have already settled on it: *City of Chappaquiddick*.

On the day of her launch, she will join her sisters in serving what is now the oldest business on Vineyard waters, older than the mainland steamship and ferry line by at least eleven years. And depending on when the rowboat ferry actually began, probably the fourth oldest on the Island itself, after an inn at the Kelley House in Edgartown (1742), another at the Mansion House in Vineyard Haven (1800 or earlier), and the Allen Farm in Chilmark (1773).

Like the commerce of the two inns and the farm, the Chappy ferry still does precisely the same job it was doing when it began. It sails to the same purpose, on nearly the same route, and with only a little more oversight or support from the town, as it did in the days of Uriah Morse, Consider Fisher, Charlie Osborn, and Jimmy Yates.

Indeed, the most outstanding and durable legacy of the service today may be the fact that in a town and on a separated island swept by two centuries of change, it is the ferry sailing between them that—in the most fundamental ways—has changed least of all.

There can be only one name for a boat as farsighted as the new ferry might turn out to be, and Peter and Sally have already settled on it: City of Chappaquiddick.

SKIP BETTENCOURT

Year-round and seasonal residents of Chappaquiddick gather for a family portrait aboard the stalwart Chappy ferries, Columbus Day weekend 2011.

ACKNOWLEDGMENTS

FROM THE FIRST DAYS OF MY RESEARCH, MOST EVERYONE LISTED IN THESE PAGES—WHETHER ON THE Island or on the mainland—recognized that the Chappaquiddick ferry was one of the great untold stories of Martha's Vineyard, and each helped me as if my research were their research and this book were their own.

I first realized that you really could write a book about the Chappy ferry when I reported and wrote a feature story about it for *Martha's Vineyard Magazine* in July 2007. My thanks to Nicki Miller (editor), Alley Moore (art director), Nancy Tutko (associate editor), and Morgan Taylor Lucero (ad designer), who have helped me research and write the book that came from that story.

At the Martha's Vineyard Museum in Edgartown, a devoted staff helped me find photographs, documents, recordings, and artifacts across the whole range of Island history. All my thanks to Dana Costanza Street (library assistant), Linsey Lee (director of the Oral History Center), Bonnie Stacy (chief curator), Anna Carringer (assistant curator), Nancy Cole (education director), and Susan Wilson (former editor of *The Dukes County Intelligencer*).

At the Edgartown Public Library, I am grateful to Felicia Cheney (the former director) and staff members Deborah MacInnis, Lisa Sherman, Alison Leslie, Donna Blackburn, Kathleen Malmquist, Virginia Munro, Elyce Bonnell, and Neuseth Clear. And to Nis Kildegaard, who scanned scores of irreplaceable photographs published for the first time in this book.

At the *Vineyard Gazette*, I thank my friends Cynthia Meisner (librarian), Jane Seagrave (publisher), Joe Pitt (the former general manager), B. J. Yerdon and Gary Cook (advertising representatives), and Steve Durkee (director of graphics and design).

Among those stalwarts and friends whose goodwill, expertise, and efforts on my behalf lend important credibility to this book, I thank Skip Bettencourt and Nancy Hugger of Chappaquiddick, Bailey Norton and Floyd Norton of Edgartown, M. J. Carpenter (a title researcher and historian in Edgartown), Ann Saylor (a genealogist and researcher in Beaufort, North Carolina), and Sara Crafts (a speedy, faultless transcriber in Oak Bluffs).

For hospitality in Los Angeles and Costa Mesa, California, I thank D. Corcoran Mellon, Buzz Tupman, and Don Ayers. And in Edgartown, my mother, friend, and lifelong cheerleader, Courtney Brady.

I am deeply grateful to photographer Alison Shaw, with whom I've collaborated on four books going back to 1996. I am also delighted to have worked for the first time with the producer and director of the accompanying short film, my fellow Chappaquiddick ferry fanatic and friend John Wilson, and his skilled videographer and editor, Scott Shucher.

I close these acknowledgments with the note that this book has been the project of my writing life. For making it possible, I will always owe my thanks to the owners of the Chappy ferry, Peter Wells and Sally Snipes, and to Jan Pogue, who with her late husband John Walter cofounded seven years ago what must be considered today among the most innovative and accomplished independent publishing companies in the country: Vineyard Stories.

—*Tom Dunlop*

SOURCES

BOOKS

Adams, "Reformation" John. *The Life of "Reformation" John Adams as an Elder of the Methodist Episcopal Church. . . .* Boston, MA: George C. Rand, 1853.

Banks, Charles Edward. *The History of Martha's Vineyard, Dukes County Massachusetts, in Three Volumes.* Edgartown, MA: Dukes County Historical Society, 1966.

Dagnall, Sally. *Circle of Faith: The Story of the Martha's Vineyard Camp-Meeting.* Edgartown, MA: Vineyard Stories, 2010.

Hough, Henry B. *Martha's Vineyard Summer Resort, 1835–1935.* Rutland, VT: The Tuttle Publishing Company, 1936.

Lee, Linsey, ed. *Vineyard Voices: Words, Faces and Voices of Island People* and *More Vineyard Voices: Words, Faces and Voices of Island People.* Edgartown, MA: Martha's Vineyard Historical Society, 1998 and 2005.

Morris, Paul C., and Morin, Joseph F. *The Island Steamers: A Chronology of Steam Transportation to and from the Offshore Islands of Martha's Vineyard and Nantucket.* Nantucket, MA: Nantucket Nautical Publishers, 1977.

Norton, James H.K., with pictures by Stevens, James G. *Walking in Vineyard Haven, Massachusetts.* Edgartown, MA: Martha's Vineyard Historical Society, 2000.

Oldale, Robert N. *Cape Cod, Martha's Vineyard and Nantucket: The Geologic Story*, revised and updated. Yarmouth Port, MA: On Cape Publications, 2001.

Potter, Hatsy, and Railton, Arthur R., eds. *Chappaquiddick: That Sometimes Separated but Never Equaled Island*, 1st and 2nd eds. Edgartown, MA: Chappaquiddick Island Association, 1981 and 2008.

Potter, Edo. *Pimpneymouse Farm: The Last Farm on Chappaquiddick.* Edgartown, MA: Vineyard Stories, 2010.

Silverman, David J. *Faith and Boundaries: Colonists, Christianity, and Community among the Wampanoag Indians of Martha's Vineyard, 1600–1871.* Cambridge, MA: Cambridge University Press, 2005.

NEWSPAPERS, MAGAZINES, PERIODICALS

Cottage City Star, Los Angeles Times, Martha's Vineyard Magazine, Nantucket Inquirer and Mirror, New Bedford Standard-Times, Steamboat Bill, The Chappaquiddick Weekly, The Dukes County Intelligencer, The Martha's Vineyard Times, Vineyard Gazette, Vineyard Magazine, Yankee.

STUDIES

Capece, Joseph. "Land-Use History of Cape Poge and Wasque." Vineyard Haven, MA: the Trustees of Reservations, 2001.

Filley, Woody, and Dropick, John, et al. "Purchase the Chappy Ferry Committee: Final Report to the Edgartown Selectmen." Chappaquiddick, MA, 2007.

Ronda, James P. "Generations of Faith: The Christian Indians of Martha's Vineyard." *William and Mary Quarterly*, July 1981: 369–394.

UNPUBLISHED DOCUMENTS

Beebe, John A. "Journal from the Barque Peru, 1847–1850" (journal, Nantucket Historical Association Research Library, Nantucket, MA).

Vincent, Hebron. "Sketches of Methodism on Martha's Vineyard, with Brief Allusions to the Early Men and Their Work, in New England" (manuscript, Martha's Vineyard Museum, Edgartown, MA).

WEBSITES

The National Maritime Digital Library: American Offshore Whaling Voyages: A Database (Edgartown): http://www.nmdl.org/aowv/whSelect.cfm.

The CPI Inflation Calculator: http://data.bls.gov/cgi-bin/cpicalc.pl.
The Inflation Calculator: http://www.westegg.com/inflation/infl.cgi.
Lat-Long.com: http://www.lat-long.com/Latitude-Longitude-616499-Massachusetts-Chappaquiddick_Point.html.

DVD

"Chappaquiddick." *A&E Investigative Reports*, DVD, directed by John Edginton. New York: Otmoor Productions Ltd. and A&E, 1994.

INTERVIEWS AND INFORMATION

These sources gave interviews or information for this book or for the story about the Chappaquiddick ferry in the July 2007 edition of *Martha's Vineyard Magazine*:

Past and present owners of the Chappy ferry as well as their survivors and descendants: Deborah Athearn, Phyd Coleman and Jean Hathaway, Skip Bettencourt and Nancy Hugger, Ann Bettencourt, Becky Bettencourt Day and Phillip Day, the late Dodie Silva, George and Priscilla Magnuson, Larry Mercier, Jerry Grant, Debbie Grant, Roy Hayes, Peter Wells, and Sally Snipes.

Captains and former captains: Jack Carbon, Bill Dunn, George Fisher, Brad Fligor, Bob Gilkes, Erik Gilley, Rick Hamilton, Keith Jackson, Jeff LaMarche, Jonathan Morse and Kim Morse, Floyd Norton, Rick Reinhardsen, Charlie Ross, Nelson Smith, Liz Villard, Matt Wetzel, Everett Whorton, and Tara Whiting.

Deckhands and former deckhands: Lucy Dahl, Caleb Enos, Steve Ewing, Molly Wells Gilley, Clara Goldfield, Maddie LeCoq, and Luke McCracken.

United States Coast Guard: Christian C. Philbrook, chief warrant officer and marine inspector.

Marine design and engineering: Captain Edward Jackson of Marine Systems Corporation in Boston.

History of the Island steamships and ferries: Bill Ewen Jr., Mark Snider, and Alissa Cafferky, a researcher at the Steamship Historical Association of America.

Vineyard and Chappaquiddick history: Chris Baer, Alan Gowell, Bruce Nevin, and the late Art Railton.

Past and present Chappaquiddick residents: Camron Adibi, Clarence A. (Trip) Barnes III, Bob Enos, Woody Filley, Ann Hoar Floyd and Tom Barrett, Cynthia and Ted Hubbard, Jerry Jeffers, Darryl and Dick Knight, Gabrielle Knight, Margaret Knight and Sidney Morris, Barry and Donna Maron, Don McLagan, Sue and Chris Phinney, David Plumb, Edo Potter, Nancy Slate and Dennis Goldin, Tom Tilghman, and Polly Wells.

Past and present Edgartown residents: Bob Carroll, Diana (Dinny) Muldaur-Dozier, Francis (Sandy) Fisher and Madeline Fisher, Carol and Dick Fligor, Dana Gaines, Bailey Norton, Eileen and Rupert Robinson, Sally Saniuta, Wendy Scandurra (Koder), and Arthur Smadbeck.

Geologic history of Chappaquiddick: Dr. Jeff Donnelly and Dr. Andrew Ashton of the geology and geophysics department of the Woods Hole Oceanographic Institution.

Wampanoags of Chappaquiddick: Elizabeth S. Chilton, chairman of the anthropology department at the University of Massachusetts, Amherst; David J. Silverman, professor of history, George Washington University; and the late Ann Coleman Allen.

Whaling from Nantucket and Edgartown: Matthew Stackpole (historian of the whaleship *Charles W. Morgan* restoration project) at Mystic Seaport; Laura Pereira (librarian) of the New Bedford Whaling Museum Research Library and Archives; Georgen Charnes (librarian and archivist), Elizabeth Oldham (research associate), and Marie Henke (photograph archives specialist) of the Nantucket Historical Association Research Library and Archives.

Theological issues: Jerry Fritz, pastor of the Federated Church in Edgartown.

History of the Uriah Morse family: David Montgomery (library assistant) at the Carteret County Public Library; Pat Edwards (librarian), Ann Saylor (genealogist and researcher), and Caroline Melke (researcher) of the Jack Spencer Goodwin Research Library at the Carteret County Historical Society; Lisa Murdough (research coordinator) and Marcia Mullins (researcher) at The Morse Society.

History of the Consider Fisher family: Barbara Gill (archivist) at the Sandwich Town Archives.

County of Dukes County Court House: Joe Sollitto (county commissioners' office); Elizabeth Herrmann, Lindsey Provost, and Daphne DeVries (probate office); Dianne Powers, Debra Levesque, Jessica Burnham, and Paulo DeOliveira (registry of deeds).

Title and probate research: M. J. Carpenter, Pat Szucs, Rachel Orr, and also Kevin Quirk of Quirk Associates of Dedham.

Edgartown town records: Wanda Williams and Karen Medeiros (town clerk's office), Pam Dolby and Kristy Rose (selectmen's office), Paul Bagnall (shellfish department), and Stuart Fuller (highway department).

Martha's Vineyard Commission: Jo-Ann Taylor (coastal planner) and Christine Seidel (GIS coordinator).

Histories of aircraft, automobiles, and clothing: Mike Creato of Classic Aviators at the Katama Airfield; Robert Stone; John Turgyon; Bill Held Jr.; and Traci-Ann DiGesu (costume shop manager), Luke Simcock (assistant costume manager), and Kathy Hood, (administrative director, drama division) of the Juilliard School.

Jaws and its sequels: Joe Alves, Jim Beller, Carrie Fyler and Matt Taylor, Carl Gottlieb, Lou and Yana Rubino Pisano, Eric Ropke.

Edgartown Marine: David LeCoq, Scott Morgan, and John D. Smith.

West Tisbury Congregational Church Bell Choir: Marsha Winsryg, Gail Tipton, Margaret Knight, and Alec Berman for help with photography.

Balboa Island ferry: Seymour Beek (president), Tom Smith (maintenance manager), Casey Jones (operations manager), Marcia Swanson (office manager), Ray DeCeco and Brad Ischinger (captains), and Blair Smith (deckhand).

ARTWORK

Thanks to those individuals and institutions who lent us artwork to consider and use in this book: Carol and Michael Berwind, the Edgartown Highway Department, Ann Bettencourt, Skip Bettencourt and Nancy Hugger, Becky Bettencourt Day and Phillip Day, Edith Blake, Laura and Tim Bryan, Douglas Cochrane, Alison Convery, Lucy Dahl, Tommy Fisher, Carol and Dick Fligor, Ann Hoar Floyd and Tom Barrett, Bob Gilkes, Cindy Grant, Debbie Grant, Sue Carroll and Jerry Grant, Roy Hayes, Chantal Hodges, Gail and Stephen Kittenplan, Margaret Knight and Sidney Morris, David and Pat Knoll, Janis Langley, Mark Lovewell, Jennifer Luce, the Martha's Vineyard Camp Meeting Association, the Martha's Vineyard Hospital, the Martha's Vineyard Museum, Patricia Mead, Roy Meekins, Larry Mercier, Meg Mercier, Jane Messersmith, Jennifer Morgan, NBC Universal, Joan Newland, the Nantucket Historical Association Research Library and Archives, Floyd Norton, Karen Osler, Sue and Chris Phinney, Edo Potter, Hatsy Potter (and Janet Holladay), Gail Rodney, Cynthia Riggs, Sally Saniuta, Ann Saylor, Alison Shaw, Mark Snider, Sally Snipes and Peter Wells, Diane Imrey Spurr, Betty and Frank Stanley, Eric Sundin, Tom Tilghman, Pat Tyra, the *Vineyard Gazette*, the West Tisbury Congregational Church Bell Choir (Patrick Phillips of www.mvartsandideas.com and Joanie Ames, videographers), and Cooper Wilson.

SILKSCREEN BY BILL ABBE/COURTESY DOUGLAS COCHRANE